I0435817

ABOUT THE AUTHORS

BETH JAROSZ is a senior research associate in U.S. Programs at the Population Reference Bureau (PRB). **MARK MATHER** is associate vice president in U.S. Programs at PRB.

ACKNOWLEDGMENTS

We gratefully acknowledge a number of individuals at the Population Reference Bureau who assisted us with this *Population Bulletin*. Linda Jacobsen provided guidance and oversight. Amanda Lee and Marissa Slowey contributed data analysis, fact checking, and help preparing figures and references. Paola Scommegna served as editor; Heidi Worley is PRB's editorial director.

We would also like to thank Joan Hermsen, associate professor of sociology and chair of the Women and Gender Studies Program at the University of Missouri, for insightful comments and advice.

The *Population Bulletin* is published twice a year and distributed to members of the Population Reference Bureau. *Population Bulletins* are also available for $7 each (discounts for bulk orders). To become a PRB member or to order PRB materials, contact PRB, 1875 Connecticut Ave., NW, Suite 520, Washington, DC 20009-5728; Tel.: 800-877-9881; Fax: 202-328-3937; E-mail: popref@prb.org; Website: www.prb.org.

The suggested citation, if you quote from this publication, is: Beth Jarosz and Mark Mather, "Losing Ground: Young Women's Well-Being Across Generations in the United States," *Population Bulletin* 72, no. 1 (2017). For permission to reproduce portions from the *Population Bulletin,* write to PRB: Attn: Permissions; or e-mail: popref@prb.org.

Cover photo: Jon Lord/Alamy Stock Photo

POPULATION REFERENCE BUREAU

The Population Reference Bureau **INFORMS** people around the world about population, health, and the environment, and **EMPOWERS** them to use that information to **ADVANCE** the well-being of current and future generations.

Funding for this *Population Bulletin* was provided through the generosity of the David and Lucile Packard Foundation.

Population Bulletin

LOSING GROUND: YOUNG WOMEN'S WELL-BEING ACROSS GENERATIONS IN THE UNITED STATES

BY **BETH JAROSZ** AND **MARK MATHER**

POPULATION REFERENCE BUREAU

VOL. 72, NO. 1

JUNE 2017

TABLE OF CONTENTS

LOSING GROUND: YOUNG WOMEN'S WELL-BEING ACROSS GENERATIONS IN THE UNITED STATES

Gains in American young women's well-being rose rapidly for members of the Baby Boom generation, but stalled for subsequent generations. Social and structural barriers to young women's progress have contributed to persistently high poverty rates, a declining share of women in high-wage/high-tech jobs, a dramatic rise in women's incarceration rates, and increases in maternal mortality and women's suicide.

In this *Bulletin*, the Population Reference Bureau (PRB) provides a broad overview of trends in young women's social, economic, and physical well-being over the past 50 years. PRB developed a new Index of Young Women's Well-Being to compare outcomes for young women (up to age 34) in the Millennial generation with young women in previous generations across 14 key social, economic, and health measures. The results show that the progress made by women of the Baby Boom generation has stalled among women of Generation X and the Millennial generation (see Box 1).

PRB's index focuses on young women who are transitioning to adulthood and—rather than only comparing women to men—compares the well-being of young women today with the well-being of women in previous generations when they were the same age. PRB's analysis calculates the magnitude of change between generations. Using this approach, we find that young women of the Millennial generation experienced a slight decline (1 percent) in overall well-being compared with women of Generation X, and women of Generation X experienced only a modest gain (2 percent) in well-being relative to women of the Baby Boom generation. In contrast, women of the Baby Boom generation experienced a substantial gain (66 percent) in overall well-being relative to women of the World War II (WWII) generation.

Women's stalled progress partly reflects growing inequality between women at the top and bottom of the economic ladder, as well as persistent racial/ethnic inequalities. Despite the decline in the national poverty rate since the Great Recession, young women are more likely to be poor today than they were in three preceding generations. Women in Generation X faced higher rates of maternal mortality than their mothers' generation, and rates are even higher among Millennial women. The suicide rate among young women is increasing, following two generations of improvement.

In addition, the share of women with bachelor's degrees is at an all-time high, but women's educational gains have not translated into corresponding gains in the workforce or in political leadership. While women have made gradual progress in reducing the gender wage gap, they still earn less than men in nearly every occupation and at every education level. In fact, women need additional years of education to earn salaries on par with men with less education. Many high-tech jobs—particularly computer-related occupations—are as gender-

BOX 1

Four Generations

- **World War II (WWII) Generation:** Born 1930 to 1945.

- Baby Boom Generation: Born 1946 to 1964.

- Generation X: Born 1965 to 1981.

- Millennial Generation: Born 1982 to 2002. (Millennials are also known as Generation Y and the Echo Boom.)

segregated today as they were 25 years ago. Women are more likely to be business owners and hold political office than their mothers or grandmothers, but they are still highly underrepresented in business and political leadership.

By looking at a collection of different measures of well-being, PRB's index provides a unique perspective on young women's progress during the past half century. The data suggest that some measures of well-being are improving, but too many women lack the resources and supportive environments they need to live healthier and more productive lives.

Fifty Years of Women's Progress

U.S. women have made significant gains overall during the past 50 years. The rise in female labor force participation has transformed gender relations, changed patterns of marriage and childbearing, and is often viewed as a key sign of women's progress toward gender equality at home and in the workforce. Between 1965 and 2015, women's labor force participation rates increased from 39 percent to 57 percent.[1] In recent years, women's labor force participation rates have declined slightly—in part due to population aging, because older adults are less likely to participate in the labor force—but women's long-term employment gains

have provided them with economic opportunities and a degree of independence not available to women of previous generations.

In recent decades, women have gained more control over decisions about education, work, marriage, and childbearing, partly because of their broader access to and use of modern contraceptives. Contraceptives became widely available in the 1960s, allowing women to better plan the timing and number of their children.[2] The oral contraceptive pill, which some social analysts credit with fueling the sexual revolution and the women's liberation movement, allowed women to plan their pregnancies.[3] Supreme Court cases such as Griswold v. Connecticut (1965) and Eisenstadt v. Baird (1972) extended legal protections regarding the right of married couples (1965) and single people (1972) to access and use contraception (see Figure 1). Male and female sterilization also gained popularity during the 1970s and 1980s, making it easier for couples to limit their family size after they reached the number of children they wanted.[4] In 2011, 70 percent of married American women of reproductive age (ages 15 to 44) used a modern contraceptive method, compared with slightly less than one-half of women in 1965.[5]

Wider access to contraceptives, combined with a rise in women's education and employment, provided young

FIGURE 1

Policy Changes Since 1960 Have Expanded Women's Rights and Protections.

Selected Policies Addressing Women's Equality, Protection, and Rights

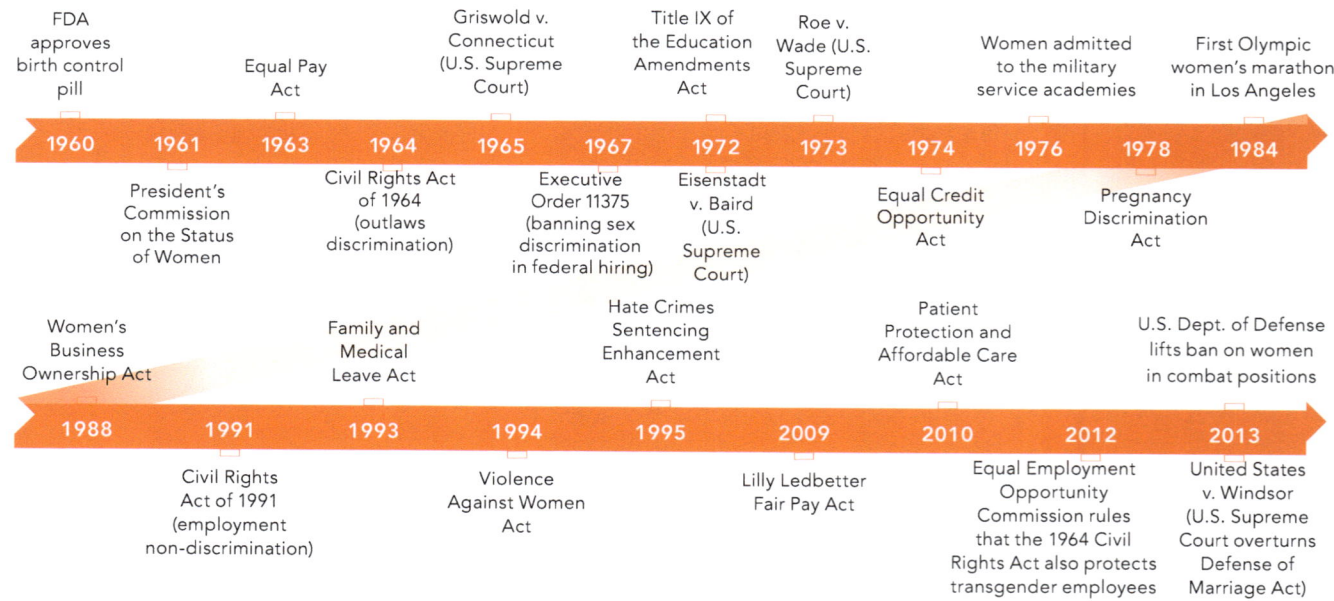

Sources: White House Council on Women and Girls (WHCWG), *Women in America: Indicators of Social and Economic Well-Being* (Washington, DC: WHCWG, 2011); and National Women's History Project, "Timeline of Legal History of Women in the United States," accessed at www.nwhp.org/resources/womens-rights-movement/detailed-timeline/ on April 20, 2017.

women with more opportunities and incentives to delay childbearing. The birth rate among 15-to-19-year-olds declined from 60 births per 1,000 females in 1990 to just 22 births per 1,000 in 2015—the lowest level ever recorded in the United States. The decline in the U.S. teen birth rate has been linked to delayed sexual activity and the increase in contraceptive access and use.[6] The birth rate for women ages 20 to 24 is also down sharply, falling from 116 per 1,000 to 77 per 1,000 between 1990 and 2015.[7]

The gender wage gap (ratio of women's earnings to men's) has also narrowed over time, partly because of the increase in women's education relative to men. A growing share of married women earn more money than their husbands—now 29 percent, up from 16 percent in 1981.[8] As more women become primary breadwinners, fertility decisions are more likely to hinge on women's earnings than they did in previous decades, which could lead to fewer births as more couples further postpone childbearing.[9]

Fifty years ago, young women were more likely to drop out of high school than young men. Over time, this pattern has reversed, with higher proportions of women than men receiving a high school diploma or equivalent degree. The proportion of women ages 25 to 29 with at least a bachelor's degree has exceeded that of young men since 1991.[10]

During the past 50 years, U.S. women have also benefited from major policy changes that have helped advance their rights and protections. Most of these policy changes were designed to protect women against discrimination in the workplace, while other policies—such as the Violence Against Women Act and the Patient Protection and Affordable Care Act—provide protections related to women's safety and health (see Figure 1, page 3).

Signs That Young Women's Progress Has Stalled

While many social and economic measures show that women have made steady progress over the past half century, a number of signs suggest that young women's progress has slowed—or even reversed—in recent years. Improvements in young women's economic security began to stall during the mid-1990s, and women's struggles have continued in the Millennial generation, particularly among women without college degrees.

Rising inequality since the late 1990s has resulted in growing disparities between women with college degrees, who tend to be higher on the economic ladder, and those with a high school diploma or less education. This growing divide has been driven in part by technological changes combined with a slowdown in the supply of highly educated workers that have increased the earning power of a college degree.[11] At the same time, structural changes in the U.S. economy have reduced real income for women and men with less education;

median earnings among full-time workers are two-and-one-half times higher among women with at least a bachelor's degree, compared with women who did not graduate from high school.[12]

Marriage rates have declined fastest among those without college degrees, resulting in a growing "marriage gap" among different educational groups.[13] Today, women with bachelor's degrees are more likely to be in stable first marriages compared with less-educated women. Among women ages 22 to 44 with bachelor's degrees, 58 percent were in a first marriage in 2006-2010, compared with 40 percent of women with only a high school diploma. Women with high school diplomas were more than twice as likely to be cohabiting (16 percent) compared with college graduates (7 percent).[14] Women with less education were also more likely to be divorced or in a second marriage.

A growing marriage gap is evident between African American and white women. In 1970, about 92 percent of black women and 95 percent of white women had ever been married by ages 40 to 44. But by 2012, just 62 percent of black women had ever married by midlife, compared with more than 85 percent of white women.[15] Declining economic opportunities for black men are at least partly to blame for recent declines in marriage among black women relative to women in other racial/ethnic groups.[16]

More than 50 years have passed since President Lyndon Johnson declared a war on poverty, but today, poverty remains pervasive in U.S. society—particularly among young, unmarried women and their children. In 2015, about 40 percent of women ages 25 to 34 in female-headed families with children were poor—about four times the poverty rate for young women in married-couple families with children (10 percent).[17]

High poverty rates among single mothers cannot simply be written off as a lack of willingness to work. Single mothers are more likely to be employed than married mothers (68 percent and 65 percent, respectively), and are more likely to be employed full time (53 percent and 49 percent, respectively). Despite higher employment rates than their married peers, single mothers are also more than twice as likely to be out of work but seeking employment (8.9 percent unemployment rate) compared with mothers in married-couple families (3.3 percent unemployment rate).[18] The majority of employed single mothers—58 percent—in 2015 were working in retail, service, and administrative jobs that typically provide low wages and few benefits.[19]

The rise in single-mother families accounts for much of the increase in women's poverty during the 1970s and 1980s.[20] In 1996, welfare reform measures led to a sharp increase in employment and a decline in poverty among women—especially single mothers.[21] However, since the early 2000s, young women's poverty rates have increased and remained at historically high levels (see Figure 2). Rising inequality is partly to blame. Women without college degrees have found it increasingly difficult to find jobs with wages that can support a family. Women of color have been disproportionately affected, partly because of their lower levels of education relative to white women.

Government safety nets have reduced the burden of poverty for millions of lower-income women and their children. From 1975 to 2007, total U.S. federal aid through programs such as Food Stamps, Medicaid, and the Earned Income Tax Credit increased by 74 percent.[22] However, married couples, older Americans, and lower middle-class families benefited disproportionately from this increase, while average benefits declined for the poorest families, especially single mothers and their children. The social safety net expanded during the Great Recession, but again, those at the bottom of the income distribution experienced smaller gains than those in higher-income groups.[23] This shift in the distribution of public funds has been attributed in part to "long-standing, and perhaps increasing, conceptualizations by U.S. society of which poor are deserving and which are not," argues Robert Moffitt of Johns Hopkins University.[24]

Despite federal laws prohibiting sex discrimination in the workforce, a gap persists between the median weekly earnings of full-time working men ($895 in 2015) and women ($726).[25] More than half of the gender wage gap has been explained by differences in the types of jobs in which women and men work, since women are more likely to work in lower-paid service and retail jobs.[26] However, the gender gap in earnings exists in nearly every occupation and at every level of education. In fact, among hundreds of occupations in the United States, there is no occupation in which women working full-time, year-round earn significantly more than men and only a handful in which their earnings are on par with men's.[27] Researchers have attributed part of the wage gap to women's roles as caregivers, and the "motherhood penalty" that mothers of young children experience through loss of job experience, workplace discrimination, and employers' perceptions that women with children are less-productive workers.[28]

Attitudes about working mothers have shifted over time, but many people still think that a mother's place is in the home. In 2016, about 27 percent of Americans still agreed that "It is much better for everyone involved if the man is the achiever outside the home and the woman takes care of the home and family." [29] The share of people agreeing with this statement represents a substantial shift compared with attitudes in 1977, when two-thirds of Americans agreed. However, most of the change in attitudes towards women working occurred prior to the mid-1990s. Since then, surveys have identified only minor changes in egalitarian attitudes about women's work.[30]

Occupational gender segregation—the distribution of women and men across occupations—declined between the 1970s and 1990s as women moved into more male-dominated jobs, and as the number of mixed-gender occupations (jobs that

FIGURE 2

The Poverty Rate Among U.S. Young Women Has Risen by More Than 35 Percent in the Past 15 Years.

Percent of Women Ages 30 to 34 With Incomes Below the Federal Poverty Level, 1968-1970 to 2013-2015

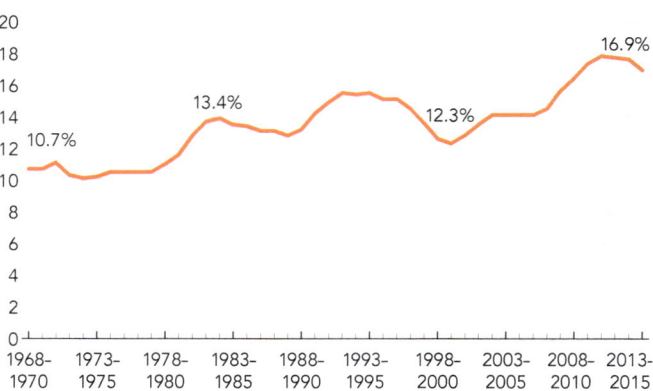

Notes: Year is year of income. The Federal Poverty Level was $24,036 for a family of two adults and two children, and $16,337 for a single parent and one child in 2015.

Source: Integrated Public Use Microdata Series (IPUMS), Current Population Survey, Version 4.0.

tend to employ both men and women) increased.[31] However, progress in reducing occupational gender segregation has leveled off since the 1990s, and women are still severely underrepresented in high-paying jobs in the natural and physical sciences, mathematics, and engineering.[32] Women currently account for nearly one-half of the total U.S. labor force but only about one-fourth of scientists and engineers. Although women have made progress in some scientific fields—such as chemistry and the biological sciences—the share of women working as computing professionals is much lower than it was 25 years ago—a trend that has been linked in part to gender biases in hiring practices.[33]

These employment and earnings gaps have translated into lower levels of wealth (assets minus debts) for women. In 2013, the median wealth among working-age, single women was $3,210, compared with $10,150 among working-age, single men.[34] Women also face barriers in accessing capital—meaning they are less likely than men to qualify for bank loans to secure a mortgage or start a business.[35]

Finally, threats to women's physical well-being have grown. In addition to a rising maternal mortality rate, the suicide rate for women has risen steadily since the turn of the century, increasing by 43 percent from 1999-2001 to 2013-2015 (see Figure 3, page 6). While the drug overdose death rate is lower among women than men, the rate for women has more than quadrupled since 1999-2001, rising to 12.5 deaths per 100,000 in 2013-2015.[36] These sharp increases coincide with the increase in opioid-related deaths as reported by the

FIGURE 3

Suicide Rates Among Young Women Have Increased Since 2000; Overdose Rates Have Risen Sharply.

Deaths Per 100,000 Women Ages 25 to 34, 1968-1970 to 2013-2015

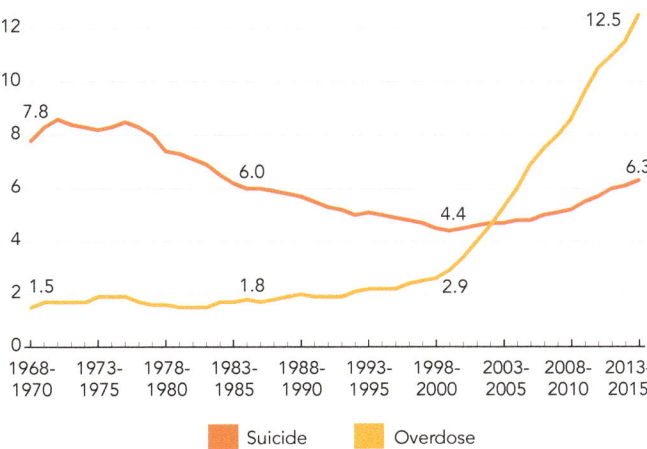

Suicide   Overdose

Source: U.S. Centers for Disease Control, National Center for Health Statistics, WONDER Online Database.

U.S. Centers for Disease Control and Prevention.[37] Rural, white women are dying at higher rates than women in other groups in what journalists Joel Achenbach and Dan Keating have called "a slow-motion crisis driven by decaying health in small-town America."[38]

The suicide rate is relatively high among white women— second only to the rate for American Indian women. However, for many key measures of well-being (for example, poverty, gender wage gap, educational attainment, and maternal mortality), African American, Latina, and American Indian women fare worse than white and Asian women. These gaps are important not only because they signal the need for policies to reduce racial/ethnic disparities, but also because the U.S. population is undergoing significant racial/ethnic change, with rapidly growing Latino, Asian American, and multiracial groups. By 2060, about 28 percent of the U.S. female population will be Latina (up from 17 percent in 2015), while the share of non-Hispanic white females is projected to steadily decline.[39]

Measuring Trends in Women's Well-Being: A Generational Approach

In the United States, women's status is often discussed in terms of the gender wage gap—how women's earnings compare to men's. However, women's status and well-being is an inherently complex topic, involving not just women's economic well-being relative to men, but also their status relative to previous generations of women across a range of

different dimensions—from education, to health, to political representation.

Are women today doing better, or worse, than their mothers and grandmothers did in prior generations when they were the same age? More specifically, were teenage and young adult women in the Millennial generation better or worse off than their female counterparts in Generation X, the Baby Boom, and WWII generations?

We focus on teenagers and young adults because women in those age groups are making pivotal transitions to adulthood and independence, including completing high school or college, leaving home, starting work, getting married, or starting families. Focusing on young adults also enables us to compare the status of women across four generations (from the WWII generation through the Millennial generation, which has just begun to reach age 35).

In order to assess changes over time, PRB developed the Index of Young Women's Well-Being. Indices are increasingly used in the social sciences to monitor trends in well-being over time, across geographic areas, and across population subgroups.[40] PRB's index combines multiple measures of women's social, economic, and physical conditions into a single measure to track women's well-being over time. (For details on the index calculations, see Appendix A: Methodology.)

The index measures were selected based on a review of the literature on women's empowerment and well-being, including resources from the United Nations and the Organization for Economic Cooperation and Development, the Global Gender Gap report by the World Economic Forum, and the California Women's Well-Being Index by the California Budget & Policy Center. These and other organizations have used indices to compare women's well-being over time or across geographic areas, but PRB's index is among the first to compare the status of women across generations. Measures were also selected based on data availability, because some relevant measures are not available for earlier cohorts of women.

Women's progress can be measured in terms of their absolute gains relative to women in earlier cohorts, or by comparing women with men. PRB's index includes a combination of measures that capture women's absolute gains (for example, in educational attainment), as well as women's gains relative to men (for example, the gender wage gap and women's political representation).

Following these guiding principles, we selected 14 measures for the PRB index:

1. **High School Dropout Rate:** Percent of women ages 16 to 24 who are not enrolled in school and do not have a high school diploma or equivalent.

2. **College Educational Attainment:** Percent of women ages 25 to 34 with a bachelor's degree or higher.

3. **Gender Wage Gap:** Ratio of women's to men's median earnings for full-time, year-round workers, ages 25 to 34.

4. **High-Earning Occupations:** Percent of workers in high-earning science, technology, engineering, and mathematics (STEM) occupations who are female.

5. **Business Ownership Gender Gap:** Percent of businesses owned by women (any age).

6. **Poverty Rate:** Percent of women ages 30 to 34 living below the Federal Poverty Level.

7. **Unemployment Rate:** Percent of women in the labor force ages 25 to 34 who are unemployed.

8. **Teen Birth Rate:** Number of births to women ages 15 to 19, per 1,000 women ages 15 to 19.

9. **Maternal Mortality Rate:** Number of deaths to women ages 25 to 34 due to "complications of pregnancy, childbirth, and the puerperium," per 100,000 live births to women ages 25 to 34. (The puerperium is six weeks following delivery.)

10. **Cigarette Smoking Prevalence:** Percent of women ages 25 to 34 who were current smokers at the time of the survey.

11. **Suicide Rate:** Number of deaths to women ages 25 to 34 due to self-inflicted injury, per 100,000 women ages 25 to 34.

12. **Homicide Rate:** Number of deaths to women ages 25 to 34 due to assault, per 100,000 women ages 25 to 34.

13. **Incarceration Rate:** Number of female prisoners under the jurisdiction of state or federal correctional authorities, per 100,000 women ages 18 and older.

14. **Legislative Representation:** Percent of legislative seats held by women averaged across two levels of government—percent of Congressional seats (House and Senate) held by women and percent of state legislative seats held by women.

Detailed definitions for each indicator are shown in Appendix B. Appendix C describes how representative years were selected to assess the well-being of each generation of women as teenagers and young adults.

By constructing an overall Index of Young Women's Well-Being, we may mask important differences among racial and ethnic groups. Comparable data by race and ethnicity were not available for all measures and all time periods in this analysis, but intersectionality—the compound challenge of multiple disadvantages—is an important facet of women's well-being. We add racial and ethnic context to the discussion of trends in women's well-being where possible. For several measures, we also note differences by educational status to show disparities between women with bachelor's degrees and those with lower levels of schooling.

Many other groups also are often socially and economically marginalized in U.S. society, including lesbian, gay, bisexual, transgender, and queer (LGBTQ) populations, women with physical or mental disabilities, and immigrants. Comparing women's well-being across all of these groups falls outside of the scope of this *Bulletin*—and data are generally limited—but we recognize that women in these groups may be doubly disadvantaged because of the unique challenges that they face.

Trends in Young Women's Well-Being Across Generations

The table on page 8 shows values for each of the 14 Index of Young Women's Well-Being measures across four generations under the subhead "Measure Values." Comparing the change in measure values from one generation to the next reveals areas of improvement (highlighted in tan) as well as negative developments (highlighted in red).

Positive trends for young women include the following:

- Women's high school dropout rate has fallen over time, while the share of women with at least a bachelor's degree has increased.

- The gender gaps in earnings and in business ownership persist, but have narrowed from one generation to the next.

- The teen birth rate is at an historic low.

- The share of young women who are smoking has dropped sharply among Generation X and Millennials.

- The female homicide rate has fallen in each generation since the Baby Boom.

- While women remain underrepresented in Congress and in state legislatures, their share of legislators has increased with each successive generation.

However, progress for young women has not been uniform across all dimensions of our analysis. Indeed, momentum in several measures of well-being has stalled or reversed:

- Women's representation in high-paying STEM occupations rose to about 1 in 4 workers by Generation X, but fell to 1 in 5 for Millennials.

- The proportion of women ages 30 to 34 living in poverty increased sharply among women in the Millennial generation compared with Generation X.

- The unemployment rate among young women fell from the Baby Boom to Generation X, but rose again for young women in the Millennial generation.

TABLE

The Young Women's Well-Being Index Measures Change Compared With the Preceding Generation.

Using the Index's 14 Measures, We Calculate an Index Value for Each Measure and an Overall Index Score

	MEASURE	AGES	MEASURE VALUES				INDEX VALUES (PRECEDING GENERATION = 100)		
			WWII	BABY BOOM	GEN-X	MILLEN-NIAL	BABY BOOM COMPARED WITH WWII	GEN-X COMPARED WITH BABY BOOM	MILLENNIAL COMPARED WITH GEN-X
1	High School Dropout Rate (Percent of Women Not Enrolled and Without a Diploma)	16-24	26.7	14.5	11.8	8.0	146	119	132
2	College Educational Attainment (Percent of Women With a Bachelor's Degree or Higher)	25-34	11.9	21.6	29.3	38.1	181	136	130
3	Gender Wage Gap (Ratio of Young Women's Median Earnings to Men's)	25-34	65.0	75.1	82.4	89.6	116	110	109
4	High-Earning Occupations (Percent of Women in High-Earning STEM Occupations)	25-34	7.5	22.7	25.1	22.5	303	111	90
5	Business Ownership Gender Gap (Percent of Businesses Owned by Women)	Any Age	4.6	26.1	27.2	35.8	567	104	132
6	Poverty Rate (Percent of Women Living in Poverty)	30-34	10.7	13.4	12.3	16.9	75	108	63
7	Unemployment Rate (Percent of Women in Labor Force Who Are Unemployed)	25-34	5.8	7.4	4.5	5.7	72	139	73
8	Teen Birth Rate (Births to Teenage Women per 1,000)	15-19	89.1	55.6	59.9	39.7	138	92	134
9	Maternal Mortality Rate (Deaths Due to Pregnancy Complications per 100,000 Births)	25-34	21.0	7.5	9.2	19.2	164	77	-9
10	Cigarette Smoking Prevalence (Percent of Women Who Are Cigarette Smokers)	25-34	43.7	32.0	22.3	17.5	127	130	122
11	Suicide Rate (Women's Suicide Deaths per 100,000)	25-34	8.3	6.0	4.4	6.3	128	127	57
12	Homicide Rate (Women's Homicide Deaths per 100,000)	25-34	6.3	6.4	4.3	3.3	98	133	123
13	Incarceration Rate (Incarcerated Women per 100,000)	18 and Older	8.9	25.7	86.1	88.8	-89	-135	97
14	Legislative Representation (Percent of Legislators Who Are Female)	Any Age	3.3	9.8	17.3	22.0	295	177	128
	OVERALL INDEX SCORE						**166**	**102**	**99**
	PERCENT CHANGE FROM PRIOR GENERATION						**66%**	**2%**	**-1%**

☐ Improving   ☐ Worsening

Notes: Values highlighted in red reflect a decline in well-being compared with the previous generation; values highlighted in tan reflect improvement compared with the previous generation. The WWII generation is not compared with the previous generation because data are not available. For the index values, when we measure percent change compared with the previous generation, values above 100 represent improvements for women, while values below 100 represent worsening outcomes. Values below 100 may be negative, depending on the magnitude of the decline.

Sources: PRB analysis of data from National Center for Education Statistics, Digest of Education Statistics; Integrated Public Use Microdata Series (IPUMS), Current Population Survey: Version 4.0; Bureau of Labor Statistics, Current Population Survey; U.S. Centers for Disease Control and Prevention, National Center for Health Statistics; U.S. House of Representatives, Women Representatives and Senators by Congress, 1917–Present; and Rutgers University, Center for American Women and Politics.

- Young women in Generation X faced higher rates of maternal mortality than women of the Baby Boom, and rates are even higher for Millennial women.

- After two generations of improvement, the suicide rate for young women in the Millennial generation increased relative to Generation X.

- Women's incarceration rates have grown 10-fold since the WWII generation.

For each measure, we calculate change in each generation's well-being compared with the previous generation (index values) and an overall index score. (See Appendix A: Methodology.) Figure 4 displays the percent change in overall index scores compared with the preceding generation. Women in the Baby Boom fared much better than women of the WWII generation (66 percent improvement or an overall index score of 166). Generation X women fared only slightly better than Baby Boom women (2 percent improvement or an overall index score of 102). However, Millennial women experienced a 1 percent decline in well-being relative to Generation X (1 percent worse or an overall index score of 99).

In other words, young women of the Millennial generation are slightly worse off today, on average, compared to the young women of Generation X when they were transitioning to adulthood. This reversal reflects the fact that women's improvements in some areas (such as educational attainment and business ownership) were offset by worsening conditions in other areas (such as incarceration, maternal mortality, and poverty). Even though slightly less than half of the measures (six out 14 measures) worsened for Millennials, the magnitude of these changes yielded the score below 100, which reflects an overall decline in well-being. Additionally, this analysis shows that much of the progress since WWII occurred among women of the Baby Boom generation—in part because of the rise in women's participation in STEM occupations and the narrowing gender gap in business ownership.

The remainder of this *Bulletin* discusses findings related to each index measure in more detail.

Women's Education Levels Have Increased

A wide economic gap divides women and men with college degrees and those with high school diplomas or less education. In 2015, median earnings for women with at least a bachelor's degree ($50,080) were nearly three times higher than those of women with a 9th-to-12th grade education (no diploma), at $17,054.[41] High school completion is important not only because it affects future earnings, but because high school graduates are healthier and live longer, on average, than those who did not graduate from high school, and people with college degrees live longer still.[42]

FIGURE 4

Progress Has Stalled for Generation X and Millennial Young Women.

Percent Change in Each Generation's Overall Index Score Compared With the Preceding Generation

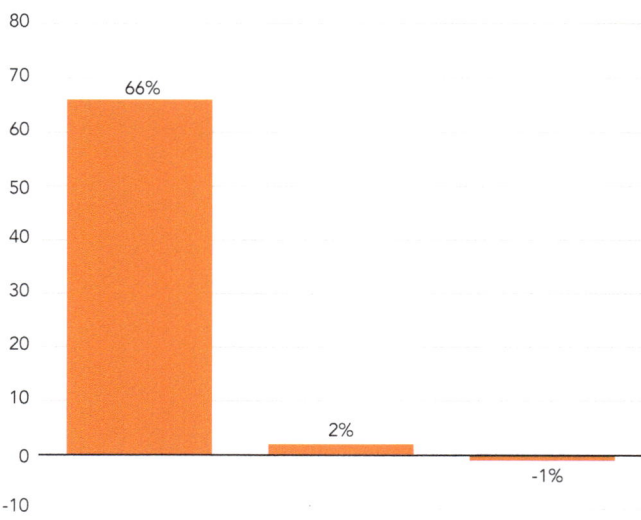

Notes: Each generation is the benchmark for each subsequent generation. WWII generation is not shown because data are not available for its preceding generation.

Source: PRB analysis.

Both young women and young men are more likely to complete high school today than in prior generations. Women in the Baby Boom generation were more likely to complete high school than women in the WWII generation, and that progress continued through Generation X and the Millennial generation. The high school dropout rate has declined for girls in all racial/ethnic groups, but Latinas have experienced the biggest improvement in recent years, helping to close the racial/ethnic education gap.[43] The growing share of Latinas who were born in the United States may partly explain their rising high school completion rates, because U.S.-born Latinos have higher levels of education, on average, than their foreign-born counterparts.[44]

Just as high school completion has risen for women, higher education has also risen dramatically from one generation to the next, and for women in all racial/ethnic groups. Among women in the WWII generation, about 12 percent of women ages 25 to 34 had completed a bachelor's degree or higher, compared with more than 38 percent of women in the Millennial generation (see table, page 8).

U.S. women today are more likely than men to enroll in and complete college.[45] However, women's higher rates of college enrollment and completion may be partly explained by the persistent gender wage gap. In 2015, women earned less money than men at every education level. In fact, women need to earn at least an extra degree to receive the same earnings as men with less education. In 2015, women with associate's degrees had lower median earnings than men with only high school diplomas (see Figure 5). Women with high school diplomas earned about the same as men with less than a ninth grade education. Women with bachelor's degrees fare much better than women with lower levels of education, but their earnings are still far below those of men with bachelor's degrees.

REDUCING DISPARITIES IN EDUCATION

Women's educational attainment has risen across the generations, but gaps remain by race and income. Among women ages 25 to 29, 47 percent of non-Hispanic white women have completed at least four years of college education, compared with 24 percent of black women and 19 percent of Latinas.[46] Given the links between education and wages as well as education and health, improving educational opportunities may be a particularly important avenue for reducing inequalities faced by minority women.

For example, girls of color are more likely than other girls to face unnecessary exclusionary school discipline (for example, suspension and expulsion), which, in turn, reduces their likelihood of future academic success. A White House report on the issue suggested that educators should work to reduce unnecessary exclusionary school discipline, with the goal of increasing young girls' educational attainment, and thus economic opportunity.[47]

Other supportive policies include universal access to high-quality early childhood education, and funding mechanisms, such as Pell grants, that assist youth from low-income families in paying for college.[48]

Women Underrepresented in STEM Jobs, Business Ownership

In 2015, women (of all ages) earned 81 cents per dollar earned by men for full-time, year-round work.[49] The earnings gap has narrowed over time, but persists for women in every age group, occupation, and education level. In 1970, young women of the WWII generation earned an average of 65 cents per dollar earned by their male peers. The gap narrowed by 10 cents for the Baby Boom generation (to 75 cents in 1985) and shrank by about 7 cents each for both Generation X (to 82 cents in 2000) and the Millennial generation (to nearly 90 cents in 2015). Among Millennial women ages 25 to 34, median earnings for full-time, year-round work in 2015 were 89.6 percent those of men's.

Part of the reason for the persistent wage gap is women's underrepresentation in the highest-paying STEM occupations, specifically computers, mathematics, architecture, and engineering. Workers in these jobs have had among the highest median earnings for the past decade.[50] Women in the WWII generation were largely excluded from jobs in science and technology (7.5 percent of high-wage STEM workers), but Baby Boom women made considerable progress—representing nearly 23 percent of high-earning STEM workers. The share was higher still for Generation X (25 percent), but then the trend reversed. Today high-earning STEM occupations

FIGURE 5

Women Need Additional Education to Match Men's Earnings.

Median Earnings Among Men and Women Ages 25 and Older, by Education Level, 2015

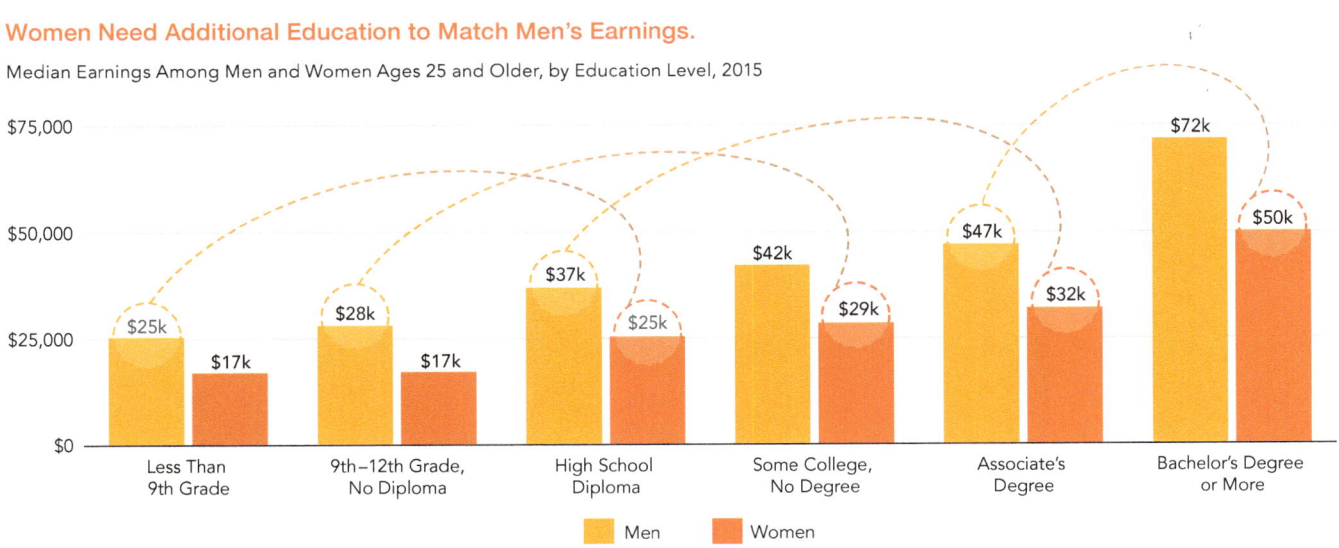

Source: U.S. Census Bureau, Current Population Survey.

are as gender-segregated as they were two generations ago (less than 23 percent of STEM workers are women).

The decline in women in computer-related occupations is especially troubling. Women in the Baby Boom generation made up more than one-third (35 percent) of those in computer-related occupations, but this share fell to just 23 percent among Millennials. This trend does not bode well for women's future earnings, since computer- and mathematics-related jobs are projected to be among the fastest growing occupations during the next decade.[51] Women are overrepresented in many other fast-growing occupations, particularly those related to health and personal care—but many of these jobs pay relatively low wages.

Minority women are particularly underrepresented among high-earning STEM workers. In 2015, African American women made up approximately 7 percent of the population ages 25 to 34, but only 2 percent of high-earning STEM workers. The gap is even larger for Latinas, who represent 10 percent of the population ages 25 to 34 but only 2 percent of high-earning STEM workers.

While high-paying STEM jobs represent only a small subset of the overall labor market, women's underrepresentation in high-tech fields is a symptom of a broader issue. Despite gains in some occupations (such as legal and military), women remain concentrated in lower-wage caregiving and service occupations, while they remain underrepresented in higher-wage occupations. Moreover, the gender wage gap persists even within occupations. Among full-time, year-round workers there is no occupation in which women earn significantly more than men and only a handful—such as counselors and special education teachers—in which their earnings are on par with men's.[52]

Women are also underrepresented among business owners. While the share of women business owners (employers and sole proprietors combined) increased nearly eightfold between 1972 and 2012, the rapid rate of increase reflects the extremely low starting point for female business owners in the WWII generation.[53] In 2012, the most recent year of data available, only about one in three business owners was female. The share was even lower among owners of businesses with employees (excluding sole proprietors); among firms that report payroll, fewer than one in five (19 percent) was female-owned.

On a positive note, the fastest rate of growth in business ownership between 1997 and 2013 was among women of color, and racial/ethnic representation across women business owners is roughly proportional to each group's share of the female population.[54]

One of the barriers to entrepreneurship among women is lack of access to the capital necessary to start or expand a business. The Equal Credit Opportunity Act, passed in 1974, was intended to level the playing field between women and men in banking and finance. Prior to that

act, credit scores were often reduced for women, simply because they were women. While the law did reduce discrimination, women are still less likely than men to have access to capital. A 2014 report to Congress found that fewer than 20 percent of small business loans (and only 4 percent of the total dollar value of those loans) went to female entrepreneurs.[55] In addition, women trail men in access to less traditional sources of funding, such as venture capital. In 2016, a mere 7 percent of venture capital recipients were woman-founded companies, and companies founded by women received, on average, 23 percent less than those founded by men.[56]

ELIMINATING THE GENDER WAGE GAP

To eliminate the gender wage gap, workplace policies must address implicit biases in hiring practices and wages. Fortunately, there are concrete steps companies and policymakers can take. For example, the city of Philadelphia recently enacted a law prohibiting employers from asking for a salary history from job candidates.[57] This policy specifically addresses the wage gap because women historically have accepted lower starting salaries than their male peers, and a low starting salary early in one's career may substantially reduce lifetime earnings.[58] Because employers may reduce salary offers based on a candidate's history, barring that information from the hiring process may help reduce gender and racial/ethnic wage disparities.

In addition, companies can limit the use of gender-loaded terms in performance reviews. Routine surveys of performance reviews find that negative terms like "bossy" and "abrasive" are often used to describe women, while critical feedback for men is framed, instead, as a suggestion for skill development.[59] While it is unlikely that policy alone could undo implicit bias, systematic review by an objective party (such as the human resources department) could identify and correct these patterns before they translate into lower pay.

Enacting family-friendly policies (discussed in more detail in the section "Reducing Poverty and Making Work Pay") could also help reduce the gender wage gap.

INCREASING REPRESENTATION IN STEM JOBS

Girls are just as proficient in math and science as their male peers. Providing additional training opportunities is one avenue for addressing women's underrepresentation in the sciences, but training alone will not eliminate stereotypes that limit women's opportunities. Social and cultural norms, which are pervasive enough that children as young as age six associate being "really, really smart" with being male, have to change in order to overcome barriers to women in STEM.[60]

Women of color are particularly underrepresented in high-paying STEM occupations. To correct this disparity, employers and educators can work together to expand access to STEM education opportunities and to develop pathways for women, particularly women of color, to pursue STEM careers.[61]

CREATING OPPORTUNITIES FOR WOMEN ENTREPRENEURS

One way to reduce the gender gap in business ownership is to maintain, or expand, successful lending programs such as the Small Business Administration Microloan Program. The microloan program backs loans of up to $50,000 for small business owners and is a key source of funding for women business owners (57 percent of loans backed through the program go to women).[62] Federal, state, and local contracting practices that provide opportunities to women- and minority-owned businesses can also be helpful.

However, business industry experts suggest that gender stereotypes also need to be addressed. One approach is through educational programs designed to change attitudes among male and female students, and encourage more girls to imagine a future career in business.[63]

Poverty Up, Unemployment Trend Mixed

While the U.S. poverty rate has fluctuated with economic expansion and recession cycles, the evidence is clear: Young adult women in the WWII generation were less likely to be poor than women in the generations that followed. The poverty rate among women ages 30 to 34 rose between the WWII and Baby Boom generations, from 11 percent to 13 percent. Women of Generation X were slightly less likely to be poor than Baby Boom women, but the poverty rate rose sharply between Generation X and the Millennial generation.[64]

About 17 percent of Millennial women ages 30 to 34 were poor in 2013-2015, up from 12 percent of young women in Generation X.

During the past 50 years, poverty has increased sharply among women without college degrees, and women who did not complete high school have been especially vulnerable (see Figure 6). Among women in the WWII generation, there was a 10 percentage-point gap in the poverty rate between young women with a high school diploma or less and women who had at least a bachelor's degree. Today, that gap has grown to 28 percentage points. In fact, poverty has risen sharply since 1999-2001 among women at every education level, with the exception of those with bachelor's degrees. An economic gap has always existed between those at the top and bottom of the economic ladder, but this gap has grown into a vast divide—separating women in terms of their income, economic opportunities, and marriage and family patterns.

Racial/ethnic gaps in poverty have narrowed during the past 25 years; however, a persistent economic divide still exists between non-Hispanic white and Asian women—who are least likely to be poor—and African American, Latina, and American Indian women. In 2015, the poverty rate among young white women ages 30 to 34 (11 percent) and Asian/Pacific Islander women (10 percent) was less than half that of African American women (26 percent), Latinas (24 percent), and American Indian women (22 percent).

Trends in women's unemployment have fluctuated over time, but the rate among young women of the Millennial generation is roughly equivalent to the rate for women of the WWII generation—at just under 6 percent. Women of the Baby Boom generation faced higher levels of unemployment

FIGURE 6

The Poverty Rate Has Increased Sharply Among All Young Women Except Those With College Degrees.

Percentage of Women Ages 30 to 34 With Incomes Below the Federal Poverty Level, by Education Level and Generation

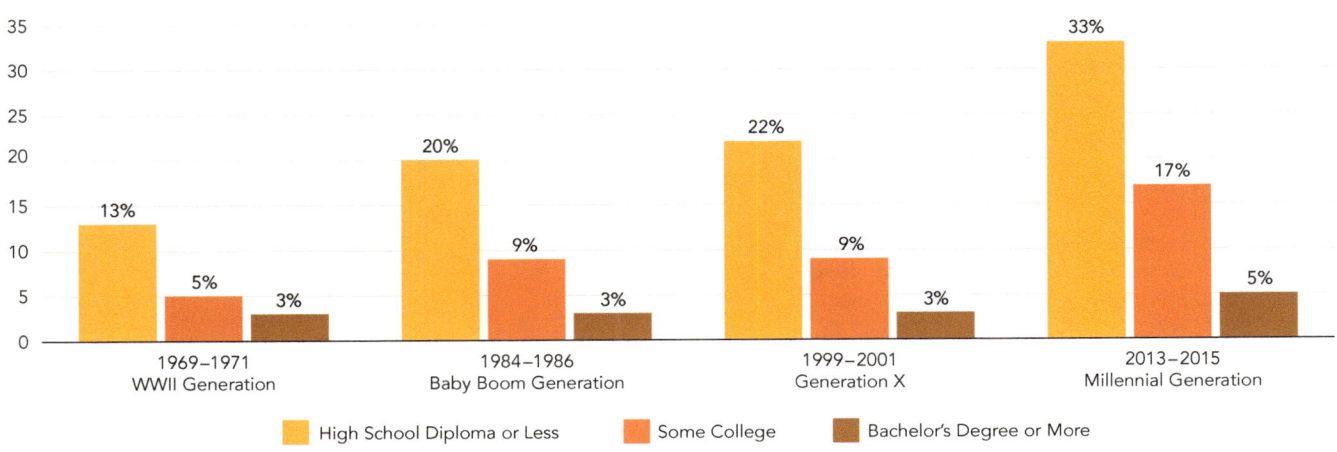

Note: The Federal Poverty Level was $24,036 for a family of two adults and two children, and $16,337 for a single parent and one child in 2015.

Source: Integrated Public Use Microdata Series (IPUMS), Current Population Survey: Version 4.0.

because they were reaching adulthood during the early 1970s, a period of economic stagnation.

REDUCING POVERTY AND MAKING WORK PAY

The poverty is higher among Millennial women than previous generations, but some policy interventions could address this troubling trend. Social safety-net programs demonstrably alleviate poverty, but (as noted earlier) married couples, older Americans, and lower middle-class families have benefited disproportionately from these programs, while average benefits have declined for the poorest families, especially single mothers and their children.[65]

For working women, several workplace practices could help alleviate poverty and reduce the gender wage gap. Policies to support an adequate living wage, an adequate number of hours (for part-time workers), paid leave, and paid sick days would provide stability and economic security for workers while improving employee retention, thus reducing costs for employers.[66]

In addition to workplace stability, flexibility is valuable to workers—especially working mothers with young children. Low-wage workers often have little flexibility and little predictability in their schedules. Simple adjustments, such as shift flexibility and scheduling practices, can have important, positive benefits both for workers and for employers.[67]

The Family and Medical Leave Act entitles eligible working women to take unpaid sick leave without fear of losing their job or health insurance coverage, and the federal Equal Employment Opportunity Commission warns employers against unlawful and disparate treatment of workers with caregiving responsibilities (whether male or female, involving child care, elder care, or other caregiver responsibility).[68] Ensuring that people can take time off to care for family is in the best interests of both the individual and the employer. While the benefits to workers may appear obvious, employers may also benefit from lower rates of employee turnover, and thus lower costs for recruitment and training, and higher rates of employee productivity.[69]

In addition to workplace policies and practices, governmental policies—especially those supporting high-quality, affordable child care—may help reduce poverty among women. Scholars point to a number of economic disincentives to work, such as tax policies and high child care costs that "make it uneconomic, and therefore less likely, that women will enter the workforce, particularly for lower-income earners."[70] Governmental programs such as Head Start and the child-care tax credit make it possible (and economically viable) for mothers to enter and stay in the labor force.

Teen Birth Rate Falls to Historic Low

The decline in the teen birth rate has been a major success story—contributing to gains in women's education, employment, income, and health. The teen birth rate fell sharply between the WWII and Baby Boom generations, from 89 births per 1,000 females ages 15 to 19 to 56 births per 1,000 females. The rate rose slightly (60 births per 1,000 women) among Generation X teenagers, but has been trending downward since then (see Figure 7). Millennials had the lowest teen birth rate of any of the four generations, and the rate has continued to fall—reaching all-time lows for several consecutive years.[71] By 2015, the teen birth rate had dropped to 22 births per 1,000 females—the lowest level ever recorded in the United States. The rate has fallen for younger teenagers (ages 15 to 17) as well as older teens (ages 18 to 19).

The declining teen birth rate is good news for several reasons. From a health perspective, teenage mothers are more likely than other women to have serious pregnancy complications, and both the maternal mortality rate and infant mortality rate are higher for teenagers than for other mothers.[72] As they reach adulthood, teenage mothers are less likely to complete high school and college than their non-parent peers, which leads to a higher likelihood of being unemployed or relying on social assistance.[73]

From 2007 to 2015, the decline in the teen birth rate has been most dramatic among Latinas, falling from 75 births per 1,000 females ages 15 to 19 to just 35 births per 1,000 females. Birth rates have also dropped for white and African American teenagers, but the declines have been smaller for those groups. The long-term decline in the U.S. teen birth rate

---

FIGURE 7

The Birth Rate Has Fallen for Both Older and Younger Teenagers.

Teen Birth Rate (Births per 1,000 Teenage Women), by Age Group, 1960 to 2005

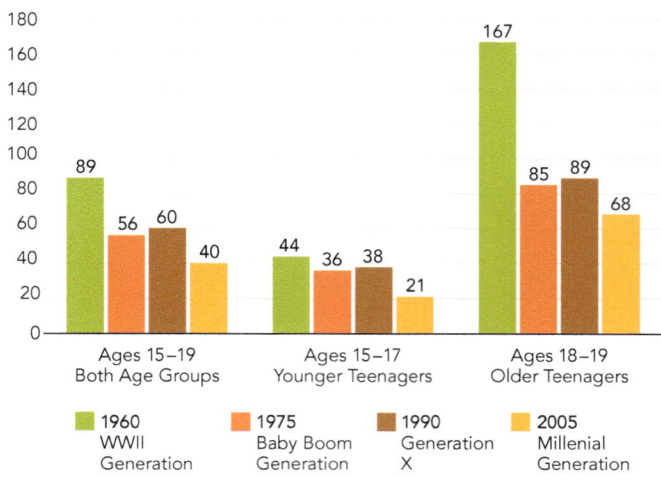

Source: U.S. Centers for Disease Control and Prevention, National Center for Health Statistics, National Vital Statistics Reports.

reflects higher rates of contraceptive use as well as higher proportions of teenagers who are delaying sex.[74]

REDUCING THE TEEN BIRTH RATE

In 2015, the teen birth rate in the United States was at a historic low (22 births per 1,000 females), but it remains high relative to other developed nations such as Canada, where the teen birth rate is 9 births per 1,000 females.[75] Policies that can further reduce teenage pregnancy and teenage births include comprehensive, medically-accurate sex education; access to family planning and reproductive health services; and access to educational opportunities.

Maternal Mortality Rising

Recent advances in public health and medicine have contributed to improvements in health and life expectancy in the United States. However, trends in maternal mortality have been a discouraging exception.[76] After rapidly improving between the WWII and the Baby Boom generations, the maternal mortality rate (the number of maternal deaths due to complications of pregnancy, childbirth, and the puerperium per 100,000 live births) has been rising. In 1999-2001, young mothers ages 25 to 34—representing Generation X—faced a slightly higher risk of death during childbirth than women in the Baby Boom generation in 1984-1986. The maternal mortality rate was also up sharply among Millennials, who faced a similar rate of maternal deaths in 2013-2015 as women 45 years earlier.

While part of the increase since 2003 may be the result of revisions to mortality data collection and reporting, these administrative changes only partially explain the recent increase.[77] By any measure, U.S. maternal mortality has increased over the past 25 years.

The increase in maternal deaths represents a major setback for women's well-being. Public health specialists consider the maternal mortality rate to be a "sensitive measure of health system strength, access to quality care, and coverage of effective interventions to prevent maternal deaths."[78] The lack of improvement in this measure implies substantial failings in the health system, such as lack of access to care and possibly inadequate treatment or discrimination in treatment.[79] These challenges may be compounded by other markers of poor health such as heart disease, obesity, diabetes, and high blood pressure.[80]

Laws restricting reproductive health services and abortion may at least partly contribute to the rising maternal death rate. During the 1970s, as abortion policies were liberalized, maternal mortality rates fell dramatically.[81] In recent years, the maternal mortality rate rose as federal and state policies began restricting access to reproductive health services.[82] In addition, improvements in fetal and infant care, designed to reduce infant mortality and improve child health, have not been paralleled by—and have sometimes come at the expense of—care for women in the postpartum period.[83]

The increase may also reflect the persistent racial/ethnic and educational disparities in maternal mortality rates coupled with growing diversity of the population (see Figure 8). Risk of maternal death is highest among African American mothers and women with low levels of education.[84]

REDUCING MATERNAL DEATHS AND IMPROVING WOMEN'S HEALTH

The U.S. maternal mortality rate is now the highest among developed nations and higher than the rate in some developing countries. Many of these deaths are preventable.[85] Policies that improve economic security are also likely to help reduce maternal mortality, as the rate is highest among high-poverty groups.[86]

While the causes of rising maternal mortality are not fully determined, health care professionals have found strong associations between women's health (and health care) and maternal mortality levels.[87] Rates of obesity/overweight have risen dramatically for young women over the past several decades.[88] The incidence of diabetes is rising among women, and diabetes is as common a cause of death among women ages 25 to 34 today (2013-2015) as it was for women of Generation X (1999-2001).[89] Rates

---

FIGURE 8

The Maternal Mortality Rate for Black Women Is Dramatically Higher Than for White Women.

Number of Maternal Deaths Related to Pregnancy and Delivery per 100,000 Live Births to Women Ages 25 to 34, by Race, 1999-2001 and 2013-2015

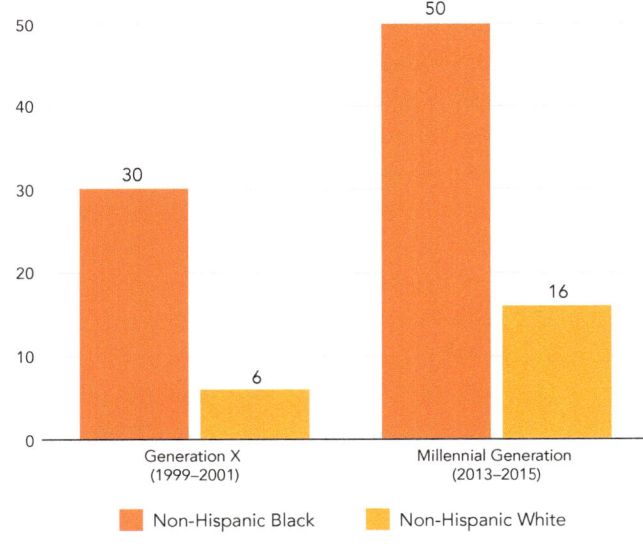

Note: The maternal mortality rate reflects maternal deaths related to "complications from pregnancy, delivery, and the puerperium." The puerperium is the six weeks following delivery.

Source: U.S. Centers for Disease Control and Prevention, National Center for Health Statistics, WONDER Online Database.

of chronic liver disease and cirrhosis have nearly doubled (from 0.7 deaths per 100,000 to 1.3 per 100,000) for young women over the same time period.[90] Each of these issues requires specific policy and programmatic interventions, but access to quality health care would be beneficial in addressing all aspects of women's health. In particular, access to family planning services and reproductive health care may be crucial to reversing the trend of rising maternal mortality.

Improvements in data quality are also crucial to understanding the causes of maternal deaths and the best ways to prevent them. Over the years, pregnancy-related deaths have been reported inconsistently on death certificates. Recently the CDC Foundation launched a new data collection initiative, the Maternal Mortality Review Data System, to provide researchers and medical professionals with better data to help identify trends in the specific causes of maternal mortality. The goal is to develop interventions (such as new screening or treatment) to combat the rising mortality rate.[91] California, the only state to have seen a declining maternal mortality rate between 2000 and 2014, has used data (through the California Maternal Quality Care Collaborative) as the cornerstone of its effort to reduce maternal mortality.[92]

Women's Incarceration Rates Increase 10-Fold

Incarceration rates have risen dramatically for women and men since the 1970s, and while incarceration rates among women remain lower than those of men, the rate of increase among women has been faster. Women's incarceration rates increased even as overall crime rates have declined. While crime levels in 2013-2015 were the same (violent crime) or lower (property crime) than in 1969-1971, 10 times more women were in prison (see Figure 9).

High incarceration rates for both men and women "cannot simply be ascribed to a higher level of crime today compared with the early 1970s, when the prison boom began," argue scholars writing for the National Research Council.[93] Rather, a combination of stiffer penalties (longer sentences) and more prison sentences per arrest have led to higher rates of incarceration. Stricter sentencing guidelines and the crackdown on illegal drugs—particularly during the 1980s—are key factors contributing to the rising incarceration rate.[94]

For many young women, a direct correlation exists between trauma and later incarceration. According to a report from the White House Council on Women and Girls:

The most common offenses for which girls are arrested include running away and truancy.

FIGURE 9

Women's Incarceration Rates Are Up Sharply, Despite Falling Crime Rates.

Incarcerated Women per 100,000 Ages 18 and Older Compared With Overall Trends in Property and Violent Crime, 1969-1971 Through 2013-2015

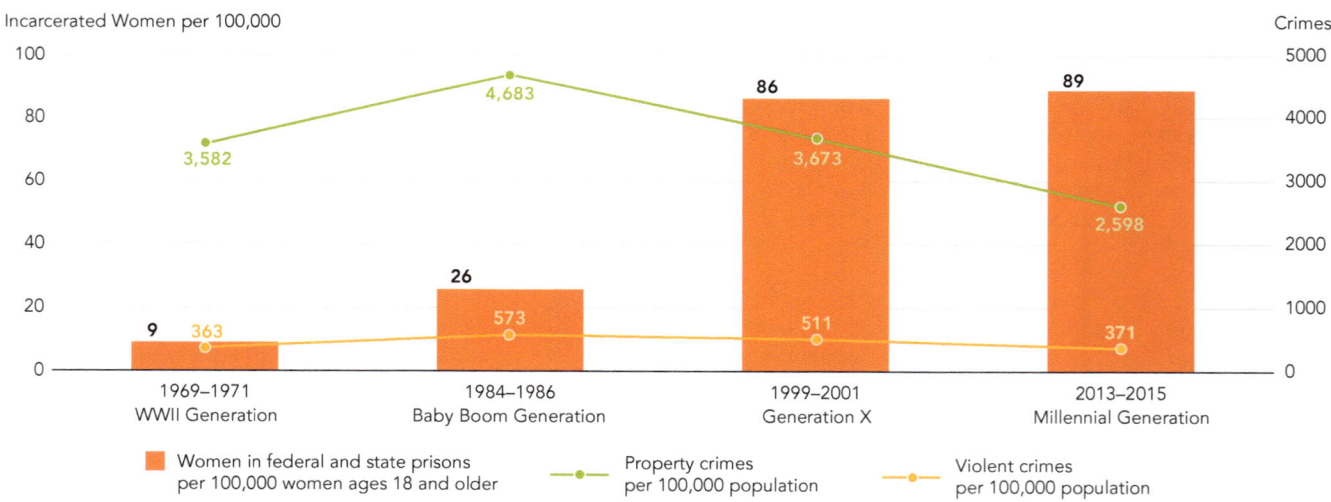

Incarcerated Women per 100,000

| | | | | Crimes |

Legend:
- Women in federal and state prisons per 100,000 women ages 18 and older
- Property crimes per 100,000 population
- Violent crimes per 100,000 population

Note: Crime rates reflect crimes committed by both men and women.

Source: FBI Uniform Crime Reporting Program and Bureau of Justice Statistics, *Prisoners Series*.

These behaviors are also the most common symptoms or outcomes of trauma and abuse. Once in the system, girls may be treated as offenders rather than girls in need of support, perpetuating a vicious cycle that is increasingly known as the "sexual-abuse-to-prison-pipeline."[95]

The incarceration rate for black women is roughly double that for white women, and the rate for Latinas is more than 20 percent higher than for non-Hispanic white women.[96]

REDUCING INCARCERATION RATES

The national opioid crisis has sparked a dialogue regarding policy response to substance abuse. In recent decades, beginning with the "War on Drugs," substance abuse has been treated as a serious crime, with stiff penalties imposed. The distribution of enforcement and severity of penalties often diverge along socioeconomic and racial/ethnic lines.[97]

Recent research suggests that treatment may be more effective than incarceration in dealing with substance abuse.[98] In response, state and local governments have begun to explore policy options to address root causes (addiction and recovery), rather than criminalize addiction.

As noted above, criminalizing trauma and abuse also can be a pathway into the criminal justice system for young women. To curtail the abuse-to-prison pipeline, victims of violence require special care. The most straightforward policy intervention for addressing the well-being of these girls and young women is dealing with trauma instead of criminalizing "status" offenses (such as truancy and runaway). Los Angeles is one of the cities that has implemented this type of supportive approach with success.[99]

Suicide Rate Increases; Homicide Rate Declines

One of the more troubling trends among young women has been the recent increase in the suicide rate. Across generations, the women's suicide mortality rate fell between the WWII and the Baby Boom generations, and again between the Baby Boom generation and Generation X, which had the lowest suicide rate of the four generations. However, young women in the Millennial generation have been more likely to die from self-inflicted causes than women from the previous two generations.

More suicide attempts do not appear to be driving this increase. Rather, young women shifted to more lethal methods of self-harm. The frequency of suffocation (a particularly lethal form of self-harm that includes hanging) as the reported cause of suicide-related death among women in their early 20s nearly doubled over the past 15 years, and the rate more than doubled for women ages 25 to 34.[100] Between 2004 and 2013, suicide rates increased the fastest in small towns and rural areas, while large metropolitan areas

experienced smaller increases.[101] Rates were highest among American Indian/Alaska Native women and white women in 2013-2015, reflecting a longstanding pattern.[102] While data for LGBTQ women are sparse, one national survey suggests that LGBTQ high school students are twice as likely to attempt suicide, compared with their straight peers.[103]

While suicide rates have risen, homicide rates have fallen. Despite common perceptions about crime trends—more than half (57 percent) of those who voted or planned to vote in the recent presidential election thought crime had become worse since 2008—violent crime in the United States has declined in recent years.[104] The violent crime rate has fallen since the 1990s and was lower in 2015 (Millennial) than it was in the 1980s (Baby Boom).[105] The homicide death rate among women ages 25 to 34 was also considerably higher for young women in the WWII and Baby Boom generations—more than 6 deaths per 100,000 women—than for women of Generation X (4 deaths per 100,000) and the Millennial generation (3 deaths per 100,000).

Over time, changes in social norms may have influenced some measures of violence against women, such as self-reported violent crime victimization. For example, in the early 1960s, professional journals and the popular press gave credence to the flawed notion that physical violence between spouses was both common and potentially beneficial to the relationship, and thus not viewed as criminal victimization.[106] Moreover, legal definitions of violence against women have changed dramatically in recent decades. Not until 1993 did all 50 states consider spousal rape a crime.[107] As a result of these subjective and legal changes over time, we focused on homicide as an objective measure of women's safety. While part of the decline in mortality from homicide/assault may be the result of improvements in medical technology and trauma care, there is reason to believe that reduced crime is also an important—and positive—contributing factor.[108]

Despite falling homicide rates, wide gaps persist between racial/ethnic groups. In 2013-2015, black women ages 25 to 34 were three times more likely to be murdered than their white female peers.[109]

PREVENTING SUICIDE

The rising suicide rate among young women is one of the most sobering findings of this analysis, in large part because the deaths could be prevented. Prevention strategies include depression/suicide awareness programs, expanded access to mental health services, and programs that support vulnerable populations (such as Native Americans, people struggling with social norms related to gender and sexual identity, veterans, and those with mental health or substance abuse problems).[110]

REDUCING HOMICIDE AND INTIMATE PARTNER VIOLENCE

While the homicide rate has fallen, any deaths due to homicide are ultimately preventable. In the case of female victims, policies and programs aimed at reducing intimate partner violence are key to reducing homicide. Women tend to be murdered by relatives or acquaintances. According to the U.S. Bureau of Justice Statistics, "In 64 percent of female homicide cases in 2007, females were killed by a family member or intimate partner," and nearly half were killed by a spouse, ex-spouse, boyfriend, or girlfriend.[111] Lesbian and bisexual women have a higher lifetime prevalence of rape, physical violence, and/or stalking by an intimate partner than heterosexual women.[112] Non-Hispanic black women face a significantly higher lifetime risk of rape, physical violence, or stalking by an intimate partner, compared to non-Hispanic white women (44 percent and 35 percent, respectively, in 2010), while the risk for Asian or Pacific Islander women is significantly lower (20 percent).[113]

Strategies to reduce intimate partner violence include teaching skills that promote respectful, nonviolent relationships; creating protective environments where people work, live, and play; and reducing economic stress on families.[114]

Cigarette Smoking Declines

Over time, a combination of public health education efforts, social pressure, and tobacco-control interventions (such as taxes on cigarettes) have contributed to a decline in the rate of cigarette smoking. Rates of current use have fallen both because fewer people begin smoking and more smokers quit.[115] In 1965 (WWII generation), 44 percent of young adult women smoked. That share fell to 32 percent by 1985 (Baby Boom), 22 percent in 2000 (Generation X), and was just under 18 percent in 2014 (Millennial).[116]

Cigarette smoking is an important indicator of health because smoking affects nearly every system in the body, raises cancer and heart disease risk, and causes more than 480,000 deaths each year in the United States, accounting for nearly one in five deaths.[117] Smoking-related illnesses cost the United States more than $300 billion each year, including nearly $170 billion for direct medical care for adults and $156 billion in lost productivity.[118]

In 2015, women's smoking rates were nearly nine times higher among women with a GED education (29.4 percent) compared to women with graduate degrees (3.4 percent). Rates in 2015 were highest among American Indian and Alaska Native women (24 percent) and lowest among Asian American women (3 percent).[119] Rates of smoking were considerably higher among lesbian, gay, or bisexual adults than among heterosexual/straight adults (24 percent and 17 percent, respectively) in 2014.[120]

REDUCING SMOKING AND COMBATTING OTHER ADDICTIONS
Public policies and media campaigns have been effective in reducing smoking rates in the United States. Further progress, targeted toward high-use communities, could include culturally appropriate anti-smoking marketing campaigns as well as cessation interventions.[121]

While a decline in the prevalence of cigarette smoking is good news, tobacco is only one of many addictive, harmful substances. Use of crack cocaine rose dramatically during the 1990s, and more recently, opioid addiction has become a national problem.[122] The death rate due to drug overdose among women ages 25 to 34 rose from fewer than 3 per 100,000 in 1999-2001 to more than 11 per 100,000 in 2013-2015.[123] All of these deaths could be avoided. Addiction prevention strategies include family-, school-, and community-based substance abuse prevention and treatment programs.[124] Preventing and treating addiction would not only save lives but may also reduce incarceration rates.

Women's Political Representation Improving but Gaps Remain

While Congressional representation has improved for women across the four generations, the measure had nowhere to go but up. When women in the WWII generation were young adults, only 2 percent of the members of the U.S. Senate and House were women. While that number has increased nearly 10-fold, the 115th Congress remains predominantly male, with only one in five female members. In state legislatures, one in four representatives is female.

This low level of representation persists despite some improvement in reported public attitudes regarding women in elective office. For example, in the 1970s nearly half of

---

FIGURE 10

Nearly One in Five Adults Still Believes Men Are Better Suited for Politics Than Women.

Percent of U.S. Respondents Agreeing With the Statement, "Men Are Better Suited to Politics Than Are Women," 1974 to 2016

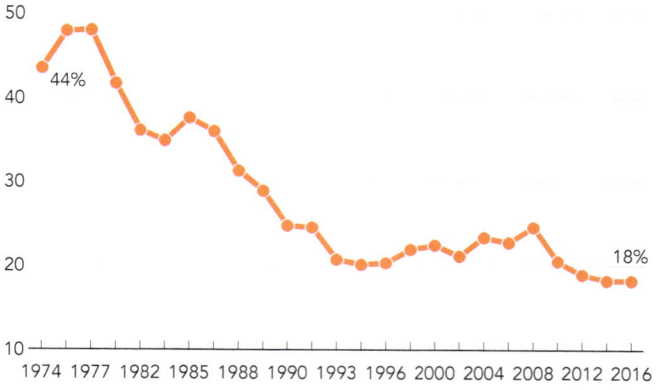

Source: NORC, University of Chicago, General Social Survey.

American adults believed men to be better suited to politics than women (see Figure 10). Today about 20 percent believe the same.

EMPOWERING WOMEN IN GOVERNMENT
Implicit bias is a considerable impediment to women running for, and achieving, elective office. An American University analysis found that women are less likely than men to think they are qualified to run for office and that they are less likely to be encouraged (by anyone) to run for office.[125] The study also found that women's traditional family/caregiver roles are an impediment to reaching elective office.

While implicit bias cannot be addressed by policy or programmatic interventions, there are organizations (for example, VoteRunLead and She Should Run) dedicated to teaching women how to run for office.

Wealth may also play a role. Running for office can carry considerable financial cost, and women have lower levels of wealth than men. Policies that reduce the gender earnings and poverty gaps may also increase women's political representation.

Conclusion

This *Bulletin* shows that young women's progress has stalled and even reversed in several key areas of social, economic, and physical well-being. Young women of color are especially vulnerable and are falling behind in school and the workforce, putting their futures at risk. Closing these gaps is critical not only to ensure that young women have the resources and opportunities that they need to thrive, but also to put the next generation on a path to success.

While this *Bulletin* examines some key components of women's well-being, several gaps in our knowledge require further exploration. For example, little information is available on the rising maternal mortality rate in the United States, or the factors contributing to the increase; yet better tracking of this measure could be an important step in reducing these deaths. For some vulnerable populations, such as LGBTQ women, data simply do not exist for most national measures of well-being, and thus issues affecting this community of women are not well understood.

PRB's analysis sheds light on broad generational trends in women's well-being as well as specific areas of progress and concern. A goal of this analysis is to provide a starting point for other researchers interested in exploring trends in women's well-being. Our approach could be replicated for states or local areas, or could be expanded by disaggregating data by race/ethnicity, education, or other characteristics. By quantifying trends and patterns in women's well-being, we can help dispel myths, stereotypes, and false assumptions about women in U.S. society—and identify potential strategies to improve women's lives.

Appendix A: Methodology

Using the individual measures displayed in the table on page 8, we quantify changes in well-being from one generation to the next. These estimated changes, under the subhead "Index Values," show how much better or worse off each generation is (or was) compared with the preceding generation as they transitioned to adulthood. This analysis involves several calculations:

- **The preceding generation is set as the baseline.**
WWII is the reference point (index = 100) for the Baby Boom, the Baby Boom is the reference point for Generation X, and Generation X is the reference point for the Millennial generation. For example, the percent of young women with a bachelor's degree or higher improved (rose) by 81 percent (from 11.9 percent to 21.6 percent) between the WWII generation and the Baby Boom generation, yielding an index value of 181 (100 + 81). The rate improved by 36 percent between the Baby Boom generation and Generation X (from 21.6 percent to 29.3 percent) for an index value of 136 (100 + 36), and by another 30 percent between Generation X and the Millennial generation (29.3 percent to 38.1 percent) for an index value of 130 (100 + 30).

- **Positive and negative change is taken into account.**
We construct the index so that values above 100 represent improvements for women, while values below 100 represent worsening outcomes. Each generation's percent increase (or decline) raises (or lowers) the index value for the measure. If improvement is a positive change in the measure (for example, educational attainment), an increase in a measure's value would result in an increase in that measure's index value. If an increase in the measure is a negative outcome (for example, poverty), an increase in the measure's value would result in a *decrease* in the index value. For example, the poverty rate rose (an undesirable outcome) by 37 percent (from 12.3 percent to 16.9 percent) between Generation X and the Millennial generation, resulting in an index value of 63 (100-37) for women of the Millennial generation.

- **An overall index score is calculated.** After constructing index values for each of the 14 measures, the values for each generation were averaged to produce generation-specific scores—the overall index score for each generation. Like most other indices of well-being, we employ an equal-weighting approach, which assumes that each measure in the index contributes equally to women's overall well-being. We chose equal weighting for two reasons. First, it would be difficult to suggest that one factor (such as educational attainment) was more, or less, important than another (such as smoking prevalence). Second, weighting criteria can be perceived as introducing researcher bias. These composite overall index scores provide a concise comparison of how women in different generations have fared over time.

Appendix B: Definitions and Sources

List of Measures and Selected Representative Years for Each Generation

	Generation and Representative Year(s)			
	WWII	**Baby Boom**	**Generation X**	**Millennial**
1. **High School Dropout Rate** (ages 16-24)	1960	1975	1990	2005
2. **College Educational Attainment** (ages 25-34)	1970	Average of 1980 and 1990	2000	2015
3. **Gender Wage Gap** (ages 25-34)	1970	1985	2000	2015
4. **High-Earning Occupations** (ages 25-34)	1970	Average of 1980 and 1990	2000	2015
5. **Business Ownership Gender Gap** (any age)	1972	Average of 1982 and 1987	Average of 1997 and 2002	2012
6. **Poverty Rate** (ages 30-34)	1969-1971	1984-1986	1999-2001	2013-2015
7. **Unemployment Rate** (ages 25-34)	1969-1971	1984-1986	1999-2001	2014-2016
8. **Teen Birth Rate** (ages 15-19)	1960	1975	1990	2005
9. **Maternal Mortality Rate** (ages 25-34)	1969-1971	1984-1986	1999-2001	2013-2015
10. **Cigarette Smoking Prevalence** (ages 25-34)	1965	1985	2000	2014
11. **Suicide Rate** (ages 25-34)	1969-1971	1984-1986	1999-2001	2013-2015
12. **Homicide Rate** (ages 25-34)	1969-1971	1984-1986	1999-2001	2013-2015
13. **Incarceration Rate** (ages 18+)	1969-1971	1984-1986	1999-2001	2013-2015
14. **Legislative Representation: Congress**	1970	1985	2000	2015
15. **Legislative Representation: State**	1971	1985	1999-2001	2016

1. The **high school dropout rate**, also known as the high school status dropout rate, reflects the percent of women ages 16 to 24 who are not enrolled in school and do not have a high school diploma or equivalent.

   Source: U.S. Department of Education, National Center for Education Statistics, Digest of Education Statistics 2016, accessed at *https://nces.ed.gov/programs/digest/current_tables.asp,* on Dec. 1, 2016.

2. **College educational attainment** is measured as the percent of women, ages 25 to 34, who have completed a bachelor's degree or higher. (Prior to the 1990s, this indicator was measured as years of postsecondary education. In those cases, we take four or more years to be equivalent to a bachelor's degree or higher.)

   Source: Steven Ruggles et al., Integrated Public Use Microdata Series: Version 6.0. (Minneapolis: University of Minnesota, 2015), accessed at https://usa.ipums.org/usa/, on Jan. 26, 2017.

3. The **gender wage gap** is the ratio of women's median weekly earnings as a percentage of men's among full-time, year-round wage and salary workers ages 25 to 34.

   Source: U.S. Bureau of Labor Statistics, Labor Force Statistics from the Current Population Survey, accessed at *www.bls.gov/cps/earnings.htm*, on Jan. 1, 2017.

4. **High-earning occupations** reflect the percent of workers who are female in computer and mathematical occupations as well as architecture and engineering occupations. These occupational categories were selected because they have had among the highest median earnings for at least the past 10 years.

   Source: Steven Ruggles et al., Integrated Public Use Microdata Series: Version 6.0. (Minneapolis: University of Minnesota, 2015), accessed at https://usa.ipums.org/usa/, on Jan. 26, 2017.

5. The **business ownership gender gap** is the percent of businesses that are woman-owned, rather than man-owned or jointly owned among business owners of any age.

   Source: U.S. Census Bureau, Economic Census, Survey of Business Owners, *accessed at www.census.gov/programs-surveys/sbo.html*, on April 6, 2017.

6. The **poverty rate** is the percent of women, ages 30 to 34, living below the Federal Poverty Level. The Federal Poverty Level was $24,036 for a family of two adults and two children, and was $16,337 for a single parent and one child in 2015.

   Source: Steven Ruggles et al., Integrated Public Use Microdata Series: Version 6.0. (Minneapolis: University of Minnesota, 2015), accessed at https://usa.ipums.org/usa/, on Jan. 26, 2017.

7. The **unemployment rate** is the percent of women in the labor force, ages 25 to 34, who do not have a job. This measure excludes women who are not looking for work, which may be a personal choice (for example, family responsibility, or to pursue educational opportunity) or because of barriers to employment (for example, lack of access to transportation or living in a community with few available jobs).

   Source: U.S. Bureau of Labor Statistics, Current Population Survey, accessed at *www.bls.gov/cps/*, on April 3, 2017.

8. The **teen birth rate** is the number of births to women ages 15 to 19 per 1,000 women ages 15 to 19.

   Sources: U.S. Centers for Disease Control and Prevention (CDC), National Center for Health Statistics, "National and State Patterns of Teen Births in the United States, 1940–2013," accessed at *www.cdc.gov/nchs/data/nvsr/nvsr63/nvsr63_04.pdf*, on Dec. 1, 2016; and "Births: Final Data for 2015," accessed at *www.cdc.gov/nchs/data/nvsr/nvsr66/nvsr66_01.pdf*, on Jan. 6, 2017.

9. The **maternal mortality rate** is the number of women ages 25 to 34 who had a primary cause of death listed as "complications of pregnancy, childbirth, and the puerperium," divided by the number of live births to women in that age group in that year, multiplied by 100,000. (The puerperium is six weeks following delivery.)

Sources: CDC, National Center for Health Statistics, "Underlying Cause of Death," CDC WONDER Online Database, accessed at *https://wonder. cdc.gov/mortSQL.html*, on Dec. 1, 2016; and "Births: Final Data for 2015," accessed at *www.cdc.gov/nchs/data/nvsr/nvsr66/nvsr66_01.pdf,* on Jan. 6, 2017.

10. **Cigarette smoking prevalence** is the percent of women ages 25 to 34 who were current smokers at the time of the survey. (The definition of currently smoking changed slightly in 1993.)

Source: CDC, National Center for Health Statistics, "Table 47. Current Cigarette Smoking Among Adults Aged 18 and Over, by Sex, Race, and Age: United States: Selected Years 1965-2014," accessed at *www.cdc. gov/nchs/hus/healthrisk.htm#cigarette*, on Feb. 21, 2017.

11. The **suicide rate** is the number of deaths to women ages 25 to 34 due to self-inflicted injury per 100,000 women ages 25 to 34.

Source: U.S. Centers for Disease Control and Prevention, National Center for Health Statistics, "Underlying Cause of Death," CDC WONDER Online Database, accessed at https://wonder.cdc.gov/mortSQL.html, on Dec. 1, 2016.

12. The **homicide rate** is the number of deaths to women ages 25 to 34 due to assault per 100,000 women ages 25 to 34.

Source: CDC, National Center for Health Statistics, "Underlying Cause of Death," CDC WONDER Online Database, accessed at https://wonder.cdc. gov/mortSQL.html, on Dec. 1, 2016.

13. The **incarceration rate** is the number of female prisoners under the jurisdiction of state or federal correctional authorities, per 100,000 women ages 18 and older. The definition of prisoners has changed slightly since 1970 but the rising incarceration rate cannot be attributed to changes in data reporting.

Sources: U.S. Bureau of Justice Statistics, Prisoners Series, accessed at *www.bjs.gov/index.cfm?ty=pbse&sid=40, on* April 3, 2017; Steven Ruggles et al., Integrated Public Use Microdata Series: Version 6.0. (Minneapolis: University of Minnesota, 2015). *https://usa.ipums.org/usa/*; and U.S. Census Bureau, Intercensal Estimates, accessed at *www.census. gov/programs-surveys/popest/data/data-sets.1985.html,* on April 3, 2017.

14. **Legislative representation** reflects the average of two measures—the percent of state legislative seats held by women and the percent of Congressional seats (House and Senate) held by women.

Sources: Data compiled by PRB from U.S. House of Representatives, Women in Congress, accessed at *http://history.house.gov/Exhibition-and-Publications/WIC/Women-in-Congress/,* on Dec. 9, 2016; and Rutgers University, Center for American Women and Politics, accessed at *www. cawp.rutgers.edu/current-numbers*, on Jan. 26, 2017.

Appendix C: Defining Generations

Years Selected to Represent Each Generation as Teenagers and Young Adults

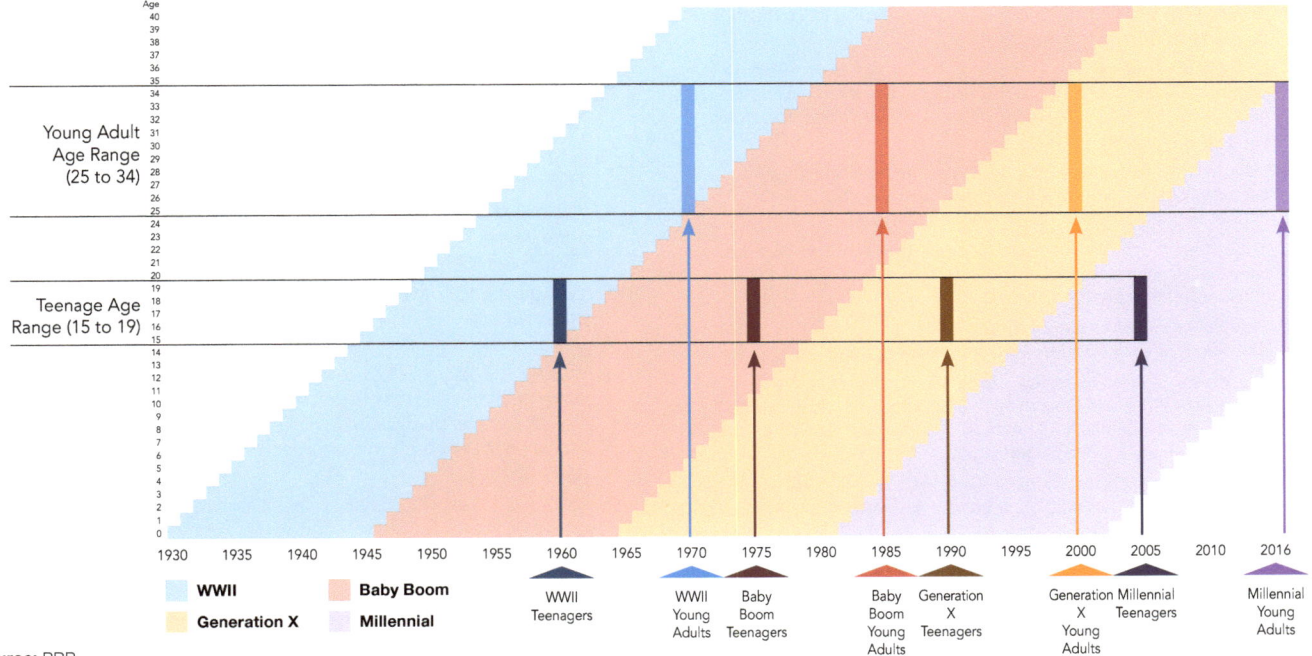

Source: PRB.

Generations (birth cohorts) span multiple years, as defined in Box 1, page 2, and illustrated in the figure at the bottom of the previous page. Because this report focuses on cohorts of young women, and each cohort spans multiple years, we simplified reporting by selecting a year that represents each generation or cohort when (at least some) women of that generation were young adults (ages 25 to 34). For example, in 1970 women of the WWII generation ranged in age from 25 to 40. Because ages 25 to 34 are contained within that range, we chose 1970 to reflect young adult women in the WWII generation. To reflect the same group of women in their teenage years (for measures such as the teen birth rate and high school dropout rate), we selected a time point 10 years earlier. In the WWII generation case, we chose 1960 to reflect women in their teenage years (ages 15 to 19 or 16 to 24 for the teen birth rate and high school dropout rate, respectively). For some measures, we selected a single year, but for many measures, such as the poverty rate, we used a three-year average to produce more stable estimates. The full list of representative years used to measure each indicator of well-being is provided in the table in Appendix B, page 19.

References

1 U.S. Bureau of Labor Statistics, "Labor Force Statistics From the Current Population Survey," accessed at https://data.bls.gov/pdq/querytool.jsp?survey=ln, on Jan. 28, 2017.

2 Norman Ryder, "What Is Going to Happen to American Fertility?" *Population and Development Review* 16, no. 3 (1990): 433-54.

3 Jon Knowles, *The Birth Control Pill—A History* (New York: Planned Parenthood Federation of America, 2013).

4 United Nations (UN), Department of Economic and Social Affairs, Population Division, "World Contraceptive Use 2016" (POP/DB/CP/Rev2016) (2016), accessed at www.un.org/en/development/desa/population/publications/dataset/contraception/wcu2016.shtml, on April 20, 2017.

5 UN, "World Contraceptive Use 2016."

6 John S. Santelli et al., "Explaining Recent Declines in Adolescent Pregnancy in the United States: The Contribution of Abstinence and Improved Contraceptive Use," *American Journal of Public Health* 97, no. 1 (2007): 150-56.

7 U.S. Centers for Disease Control and Prevention (CDC), National Center for Health Statistics, "Vital Statistics of the United States 1990. Volume I - Natality," accessed at www.cdc.gov/nchs/data/vsus/nat90_1acc.pdf, on May 26, 2017; and CDC, National Center for Health Statistics, "Births: Final Data for 2015," (2017) accessed at www.cdc.gov/nchs/data/nvsr/nvsr66/nvsr66_01.pdf, on Jan. 6, 2017.

8 U.S. Census Bureau, "Table F-22, Married-Couple Families With Wives' Earnings Greater Than Husbands' Earnings," accessed at www.census.gov/data/tables/time-series/demo/income-poverty/historical-income-families.html, on Jan. 28, 2017.

9 Mark Mather, "Fact Sheet: The Decline in U.S. Fertility" (July 2012), accessed at www.prb.org/publications/datasheets/2012/world-population-data-sheet/fact-sheet-us-population.aspx, on April 18, 2017.

10 Kelvin Pollard, "The Gender Gap in College Enrollment and Graduation" (April 2011), accessed at www.prb.org/Publications/Articles/2011/gender-gap-in-education.aspx, on April 20, 2017.

11 Claudia Goldin and Lawrence F. Katz, *The Race Between Education and Technology* (Cambridge, MA: Harvard University Press, 2009).

12 U.S. Bureau of Labor Statistics, "Table 17: Median Usual Weekly Earnings of Full-Time Wage and Salary Workers 25 Years and Older, by Educational Attainment and Gender, 2014 Annual Averages," in "Women in the Labor Force: A Databook," BLS Reports 1059 (2015): 62.

13 Mark Mather and Diana Lavery, "In U.S., Proportion Married at Lowest Recorded Levels" (Sept. 2010), accessed at www.prb.org/Articles/2010/usmarriagedecline.aspx, on April 20, 2017.

14 Casey E. Copen et al., "First Marriages in the United States: Data From the 2006-2010 National Survey of Family Growth," *National Health Statistics Reports* 49 (2012).

15 R. Kelly Raley, Megan M. Sweeney, and Danielle Wondra, "The Growing Racial and Ethnic Divide in U.S. Marriage Patterns," *The Future of Children* 25, no. 2 (2015): 89-109.

16 William Julius Wilson, *The Truly Disadvantaged: The Inner City, the Underclass, and Public Policy* (Chicago: University of Chicago Press, 1987).

17 U.S. Census Bureau, Current Population Survey, "POV03: People in Families With Related Children Under 18 by Family Structure, Age, and Sex, Iterated by Income-to-Poverty Ratio and Race: 2015 Below 100% of Poverty–All Races," accessed at www.census.gov/data/tables/time-series/demo/income-poverty/cps-pov/pov-03.html, on April 19, 2017.

18 U.S. Bureau of Labor Statistics, "Table 5. Employment Status of the Population by Sex, Marital Status, and Presence and Age of Own Children Under 18, 2014-2015 Annual Averages," accessed at www.bls.gov/news.release/archives/famee_04222016.htm, on June 2, 2017.

19 PRB analysis of data from the U.S. Census Bureau, 2016 Current Population Survey.

20 John Iceland, *Poverty in America: A Handbook* (Oakland, CA: University of California Press, 2003).

21 Daniel T. Lichter and Martha L. Crowley, "Poverty in America: Beyond Welfare Reform," *Population Bulletin* 57, no. 2 (2002).

22 Johns Hopkins University, "U.S. Welfare Spending Up — But Help for the Neediest Down," accessed at http://releases.jhu.edu/2014/05/06/u-s-welfare-spending-up-but-help-for-the-neediest-down/, on June 2, 2017.

23 Robert Moffitt, "The Great Recession and the Social Safety Net," *The Annals of the American Academy of Political and Social Science* 650, no. 1 (2016): 143-66.

24 Moffitt, "The Deserving Poor, the Family, and the U.S. Welfare System."

25 U.S. Bureau of Labor Statistics, "Highlights of Women's Earnings in 2015," *BLS Reports* 1064 (2016).

26 Francine D. Blau and Lawrence M. Kahn, "The Gender Pay Gap: Have Women Gone as Far as They Can?" *Academy of Management Perspectives* 21, no. 1 (2007): 7-23.

27 Beth Jarosz, "Occupational Earnings Gap" (Dec. 2015), accessed at www.prb.org/Multimedia/Infographics/2015/tableau-gender-wage-gap.aspx, on Jan. 9, 2017.

28 Michelle J. Budig and Paula England, "The Wage Penalty for Motherhood," *American Sociological Review* 66, no. 2 (2001): 204-25; and Shelley J. Correll, Stephen Benard, and In Paik, "Getting a Job: Is There a Motherhood Penalty?" *American Journal of Sociology* 112, no. 5 (2007): 1297-339.

29 GSS Data Explorer, accessed at https://gssdataexplorer.norc.org, on April 20, 2017.

30 David Cotter, Joan M. Hermsen, and Reeve Vanneman, "The End of the Gender Revolution? Gender Role Attitudes From 1977 to 2008," *American Journal of Sociology* 117, no. 1 (2011): 259-89.

31 Ariane Hegewisch and Heidi Hartmann, *Occupational Segregation and the Gender Wage Gap: A Job Half Done* (Washington, DC: Institute for Women's Policy Research, 2014).

32 David A. Cotter, Joan M. Hermsen, and Reeve Vanneman, "Gender Inequality at Work," in *The American People: Census 2000*, ed. Reynolds Farley and John Haaga (New York: Russell Sage Foundation, 2005).

33 American Association of University Women (AAUW), *Solving the Equation: The Variables for Women's Success in Engineering and Computing* (Washington, DC: AAUW, 2015).

34 Erin Ruel and Robert M. Hauser, "Explaining the Gender Wealth Gap," *Demography* 50, no. 4 (2013): 1155-76; and Mariko Chang, *Women and Wealth: Insights for Grantmakers* (2015), accessed at http://assetfunders.org/images/pages/AFN_Women_and_Wealth_Brief_2015.pdf, on May 11, 2017.

35 U.S. Senate, Committee on Small Business and Entrepreneurship, "21st Century Barriers to Women's Entrepreneurship," Majority Report of the U.S. Senate Committee on Small Business and Entrepreneurship, July 23, 2014, accessed at www.sbc.senate.gov/public/?a=Files.Serve&File_id=3f954386-f16b-48d2-86ad-698a75e33cc4, on May 11, 2017.

36 While the rising rate of deaths related to drug overdose is important to women's well-being, it is one of several mortality measures not included in the PRB Index of Young Women's Well-Being. The three mortality measures included in the PRB Index are maternal mortality, homicide, and suicide based on literature showing that they represent measures of health care, safety, and emotional well-being, respectively.

37 Rose A. Rudd et al., "Increases in Drug and Opioid Overdose Deaths–United States, 2000-2014," *Morbidity and Mortality Weekly Report* 64, no. 50 (2016): 1378-82.

38 Joel Achenbach and Dan Keating, "A New Divide in American Death," *The Washington Post,* April 10, 2016.

39 U.S. Census Bureau, "Annual Estimates of the Resident Population by Sex, Age, Race, and Hispanic Origin for the United States: April 1, 2010 to July 1, 2015," accessed at www.census.gov/data/tables/2015/demo/popest/nation-detail.html, on May 5, 2017; and U.S. Census Bureau, "Table 10. Projections of the Population by Sex, Hispanic Origin, and Race for the United States: 2015 to 2060," accessed at www.census.gov/population/projections/data/national/2014/summarytables.html, on May 4, 2017.

40 Justin Fox, "The Economics of Well Being," *Harvard Business Review*, Jan.-Feb. 2012.

41 U.S. Census Bureau, "Table P-20. Educational Attainment–Workers 25 Years Old and Over by Median Earnings and Sex: 1991 to 2015," accessed at www.census.gov/data/tables/time-series/demo/income-poverty/historical-income-people.html, on April 19, 2017.

42 Robert A. Hummer and Elaine M. Hernandez, "The Effect of Educational Attainment on Adult Mortality in the United States," *Population Bulletin* 68, no. 1 (2013).

43 Girl Scout Research Institute, "The State of Girls 2017: Emerging Truths and Troubling Trends," accessed at www.girlscouts.org/content/dam/girlscouts-gsusa/forms-and-documents/about-girl-scouts/research/GSUSA_State-of-Girls-Report_2017.pdf, on May 4, 2017.

44 Mark Mather and Patricia Foxen, *Toward A More Equitable Future: The Trends and Challenges Facing America's Latino Children* (Washington, DC: National Council of La Raza, 2016).

45 PRB, "The Decline in U.S. Fertility," (Dec. 2014), accessed at www.prb.org/Publications/Datasheets/2014/2014-world-population-data-sheet/us-fertility-decline-factsheet.aspx, on June 2, 2017.

46 U.S. Census Bureau, Current Population Survey, "Table A-2: Percent of People 25 Years and Over Who Have Completed High School or College, by Race, Hispanic Origin, and Sex: Selected Years 1940 to 2015," accessed at www.census.gov/data/tables/time-series/demo/educational-attainment/cps-historical-time-series.html, on April 17, 2017.

47 The White House Council on Women and Girls, *Advancing Equity for Women and Girls of Color* (Washington, DC: The White House, 2015).

48 U.S. Department of Education, "Equity of Opportunity," accessed at www.ed.gov/equity, on Feb. 27, 2017.

49 U.S. Bureau of Labor Statistics, "Highlights of Women's Earnings in 2015."

50 Data on occupational earnings were drawn from the American Community Survey 2005 and 2015. Legal occupations also ranked in the top three high-earning occupations, along with computer, mathematics, architecture, and engineering, but are not included because they are not considered science, technology, engineering, or mathematics jobs.

51 U.S. Bureau of Labor Statistics, "Projections of Occupational Employment, 2014-24" (Dec. 2015), accessed at www.bls.gov/careeroutlook/2015/article/projections-occupation.htm, on April 20, 2017.

52 Jarosz, "Occupational Earnings Gap."

53 U.S. Census Bureau, Economic Census, Survey of Business Owners, accessed at www.census.gov/programs-surveys/sbo.html, on April 6, 2017.

54 American Express OPEN, "The 2013 State of Women-Owned Business Report: A Summary of Important Trends, 1997-2013" (2013), accessed at www.womenable.com/content/userfiles/2013_State_of_Women-Owned_Businesses_Report_FINAL.pdf, on May 11, 2017.

55 Kenneth Temkin, Brett Theodos, and Kerstin Gentsch (Jan. 2008), "Competitive and Special Competitive Opportunity Gap Analysis of the 7(a) and 504 Programs," accessed at www.urban.org/research/publication/competitive-and-special-competitive-opportunity-gap-analysis-7a-and-504-programs/view/full_report, on June 2, 2017.

56 Laurie Meisler, Mira Rojanasakul, and Jeremy Scott Diamond, "Who Gets Venture Capital Funding?" *Bloomberg*, May 25, 2016, accessed at www.bloomberg.com/graphics/2016-who-gets-vc-funding/, on April 6, 2017.

57 Tricia L. Nadolny, "Your Salary Will Soon be Your Secret in Philadelphia," Dec. 8, 2016, accessed at www.philly.com, on April 19, 2017.

58 Adrienne Dawson, "Why Do Women Accept Lower Salary Offers Than Men?" April 29, 2014, accessed at www.texasenterprise.utexas.edu/2014/04/28/leadership/why-do-women-accept-lower-salary-offers-men, on Feb. 2, 2017; Kerri Anne Renzulli, "The Costly Career Mistake Millennials Are Making," *Time Magazine*, May 14, 2015; and Fatih Guvenen et al., "What Do Data on Millions of U.S. Workers Reveal About Life-Cycle Earnings Risk?" *Federal Reserve Bank of New York Staff Reports* 710 (2015).

59 Kieran Snyder, "The Abrasiveness Trap: High-Achieving Men and Women Are Described Differently in Reviews" *Fortune*, Aug. 26, 2014, accessed at http://fortune.com/2014/08/26/performance-review-gender-bias/, on Feb. 2, 2017.

60 Ed Yong, "6-Year-Old Girls Already Have Gendered Beliefs About Intelligence," *The Atlantic,* Jan. 26, 2017, accessed at www.theatlantic.com/science/archive/2017/01/six-year-old-girls-already-have-gendered-beliefs-about-intelligence/514340/, on Feb. 2, 2017.

61 The White House Council on Women and Girls, *Advancing Equity for Women and Girls of Color.*

62 U.S. Senate, Committee on Small Business and Entrepreneurship, "21st Century Barriers to Women's Entrepreneurship."

63 Scott Shane, "Closing the Business-Ownership Gender Gap," *Entrepreneur*, Jan. 29, 2014, accessed at www.entrepreneur.com/article/231115, on April 6, 2017.

64 The poverty rate shows the percent of women, ages 30 to 34, living below the Federal Poverty Level. We selected ages 30 to 34 for this indicator to ensure that our analysis was not influenced by the effects of rising college enrollment (college-enrolled students are more likely to be listed as in poverty—while enrolled—than their same-age, unenrolled peers).

65 Moffitt, "The Deserving Poor, the Family, and the U.S. Welfare System."

66 U.S. Department of Labor, Women's Bureau, "Workplace Flexibility: Information and Options for Small Businesses" (Oct. 2015), accessed at www.dol.gov/wb/resources/, on Jan. 23, 2017.

67 U.S. Department of Labor, Women's Bureau, "Workplace Flexibility: Information and Options for Small Businesses."

68 U.S. Equal Employment Opportunity Commission, "Enforcement Guidance: Unlawful Disparate Treatment of Workers With Caregiving Responsibilities" (May 2007), accessed at www.eeoc.gov/policy/docs/caregiving.html, on April 19, 2017.

69 Laurie Tarkan, "The Benefits of Flextime (to Employers)," July 22, 2011, accessed at www.cbsnews.com/news/the-benefits-of-flextime-to-employers/, on April 19, 2017; Stephen Miller, "Parents Rank Flextime Benefits Ahead of Salary," Aug. 17, 2016, accessed at www.shrm.org/resourcesandtools/hr-topics/benefits/pages/parents-rank-flextime-above-salary.aspx, on April 19, 2017; Nevada State Bank, "The Ups and Downs of Flex Time," accessed at https://nevadasmallbusiness.com/the-advantages-and-disadvantages-of-flex-time/, on April 19, 2017; and David G. Javitch, "The Benefits of Flextime," *Entrepreneur*, June 5, 2006, accessed at www.entrepreneur.com/article/159440, on April 19, 2017.

70 Heidi Crebo-Rediker et al., "Women in the Economy: Global Growth Generators," *Citi Global Perspectives and Solutions Report Series*, no. 35 (2015) accessed at www.cfr.org/content/publications/Women_in_the_Economy.pdf, on May 11, 2017.

71 Heidi Worley, "Teen Births Continue to Decline in U.S." (June 2014), accessed at www.prb.org/Publications/Articles/2014/us-teen-births.aspx, on Jan. 9, 2017.

72 Ashok Kumar et al., "Outcome of Teenage Pregnancy," *The Indian Journal of Pediatrics* 74, no. 10 (2007): 927-31.

73 Interagency Working Group on Youth Programs, "Pregnancy Prevention, Adverse Effects," accessed at http://youth.gov/youth-topics/teen-pregnancy-prevention/adverse-effects-teen-pregnancy, on Feb. 12, 2017.

74 Santelli et al., "Explaining Recent Declines in Adolescent Pregnancy in the United States."

75 CDC, National Center for Health Statistics, "Births: Final Data for 2015," accessed at www.cdc.gov/nchs/data/nvsr/nvsr66/nvsr66_01.pdf, on May 16, 2017; and World Bank, "Adolescent Fertility Rate (Births per 1,000 Women Ages 15-19)," accessed at http://data.worldbank.org/indicator/SP.ADO.TFRT?locations=GB-CA-US-FR-DE, on May 16, 2017.

76 To provide comparable data over time for all generations, the maternal mortality measure used in this report is based on the number of women ages 25 to 34 who had a primary cause of death listed as "Complications of pregnancy, childbirth, and the puerperium." The number of maternal deaths is divided by the number of live births to young women in that year, and the ratio is shown per 100,000 births. Starting in 1986, the CDC began a new program for monitoring pregnancy-related mortality. That report shows a lower level of mortality for recent years, but both measures show an upward trend since 1987. We use the rate based on complications of pregnancy, childbirth, and the puerperium so that we have comparable data prior to 1987, and so that we can limit the analysis to women ages 25 to 34.

77 Elliot K. Main, "Maternal Mortality: New Strategies for Measurement and Prevention," *Current Opinion in Obstetrics and Gynecology* 22, no. 6 (2010): 511-16; and Marian F. MacDorman et al., "Recent Increases in the U.S. Maternal Mortality Rate: Disentangling Trends From Measurement Issues," *Obstetrics and Gynecology* 128, no. 3 (2016): 447-55.

78 Save the Children, *The Urban Disadvantage: State of the World's Mothers 2015* (Fairfield, CT: Save the Children Federation, 2015).

79 Amnesty International, *Deadly Delivery: The Maternal Health Care Crisis in the USA* (London: Amnesty International Secretariat, 2010).

80 William M. Callaghan, "Overview of Maternal Mortality in the United States," *Seminars in Perinatology* 36, no. 1 (2012): 2-6; and Catherine Spong et al., interview with Diane Rehm, *The Diane Rehm Show*, 88.5 WAMU FM, Oct. 12, 2016, accessed at http://thedianerehmshow.org/shows/2016-10-12/whats-behind-increase-in-the-u-s-maternal-death-rate, on Feb. 10, 2017.

81 "Liberal State Abortion Laws Affect Maternal Mortality," *Health Services Reports* 87, no. 5 (1972): 419-21.

82 "How America's Abortion Laws Have Changed," *The Economist*, May 2, 2016, accessed at www.economist.com/blogs/economist-explains/2016/03/economist-explains-0, on May 4, 2017; and Elizabeth Nash et al., "Policy Trends in the States: 2016," Guttmacher Institute Policy Analysis (Jan. 2017), accessed at www.guttmacher.org/article/2017/01/policy-trends-states-2016, on May 4, 2017.

83 Nina Martin and Renee Montagne, "Focus On Infants During Childbirth Leaves U.S. Moms In Danger," May 12, 2017, accessed at www.npr.org/2017/05/12/527806002/focus-on-infants-during-childbirth-leaves-u-s-moms-in-danger, on May 16, 2017.

84 American College of Obstetricians and Gynecologists, "Racial and Ethnic Disparities in Obstetrics and Gynecology," Committee Opinion no. 649 (2015), accessed at www.acog.org/Resources-And-Publications/Committee-Opinions/Committee-on-Health-Care-for-Underserved-Women/Racial-and-Ethnic-Disparities-in-Obstetrics-and-Gynecology, on May 8, 2017.

85 Ina May Gaskin, "Maternal Death in the United States: A Problem Solved or a Problem Ignored?" *The Journal of Perinatal Education* 17, no. 2 (2008): 9-13.

86 Gopal K. Singh, *Maternal Mortality in the United States, 1935-2007: Substantial Racial/Ethnic, Socioeconomic, and Geographic Disparities Persist* (Rockville, MD: U.S. Department of Health and Human Services, 2010).

87 Michael A. Schellpfeffer et al., "A Review of Pregnancy-Related Maternal Mortality in Wisconsin, 2006-2010," *WMJ* 114, no. 5 (2015): 202-7.

88 CDC, National Center for Health Statistics, "Health, United States, 2015– Health Risk Factors" (April 2016), accessed at www.cdc.gov/nchs/hus/healthrisk.htm, on April 19, 2017.

89 CDC, "Age-Adjusted Incidence of Diagnosed Diabetes per 1,000 Population Aged 18-79 Years, by Sex, United States, 1980-2014" (Dec., 2015), accessed at www.cdc.gov/diabetes/statistics/incidence/fig4.htm, on April 19, 2017; and CDC, "CDC, National Center for Health Statistics, CDC WONDER Online Database," accessed at https://wonder.cdc.gov/, on April 20, 2017.

90 CDC, "CDC WONDER Online Database."

91 CDC Foundation, "CDC Foundation Partnership to Help Reduce Maternal Mortality in the United States," April 19, 2016, accessed at www.cdcfoundation.org/pr/2016/cdc-foundation-partnership-help-reduce-maternal-mortality-united-states, on April 19, 2017.

92 MacDorman et al., "Recent Increases in the U.S. Maternal Mortality Rate: Disentangling Trends From Measurement Issues."

93 National Research Council (NRC), "Rising Incarceration Rates," in *The Growth of Incarceration in the United States: Exploring Causes and Consequences*, ed. Jeremy Travis, Bruce Western, and Steve Redburn (Washington, DC: The National Academies Press, 2014).

94 NRC, "Rising Incarceration Rates."

95 The White House Council on Women and Girls, *Advancing Equity for Women and Girls of Color*.

96 E. Ann Carson and Elizabeth Anderson, "Prisoners in 2015," U.S. Department of Justice, Office of Justice Programs, Bureau of Justice Statistics, Bulletin NCJ 250229 (Dec. 2016).

97 William J. Stuntz, "Race, Class, and Drugs," *Columbia Law Review* 98, no. 7 (1998): 1795-842.

98 Gary A. Zarkin et al., "Lifetime Benefits and Costs of Diverting Substance-Abusing Offenders From State Prison," *Crime and Delinquency* 61, no. 6 (2015): 829-50.

99 CBS Los Angeles, "Police and Nonprofit Team Up to End Sex Trafficking," Feb. 7, 2017, accessed at http://losangeles.cbslocal.com/2017/02/07/police-and-nonprofit-team-up-to-end-sex-trafficking/, on April 19, 2017.

100 Beth Jarosz and Alicia VanOrman, "Accidental Poisoning Deaths—Mostly Drug Overdoses—Exceed Homicides of U.S. Young Adults" (Feb. 2016), accessed at www.prb.org/Publications/Articles/2016/young-adult-suicide.aspx, on Jan. 9, 2017; and CDC, National Center for Health Statistics, "Underlying Cause of Death," CDC WONDER Online Database, accessed at https://wonder.cdc.gov/mortSQL.html, on May 16, 2017.

101 Li-Hui Chen and Deborah D. Ingram, "QuickStats: Age-Adjusted Rates for Suicide, by Urbanization of County of Residence–United States, 2004 and 2013," *Morbidity and Mortality Weekly Report* 64, no. 14 (2015): 401.

102 CDC, CDC WONDER Online Database, "Underlying Cause of Death 1999-2015" (Dec. 2016), accessed at http://wonder.cdc.gov/ucd-icd10.html, on Feb. 17, 2017. Data are from the Multiple Cause of Death Files, 1999-2015, as compiled from data provided by the 57 vital statistics jurisdictions through the Vital Statistics Cooperative Program.

103 CDC, "LGBT Youth," Nov. 12, 2014, accessed at www.cdc.gov/lgbthealth/youth.htm, on April 19, 2017.

104 John Gramlich, "Voters' Perceptions of Crime Continue to Conflict With Reality," Nov. 16, 2016, accessed at www.pewresearch.org/fact-tank/2016/11/16/voters-perceptions-of-crime-continue-to-conflict-with-reality/, on April 19, 2017.

105 U.S. Department of Justice, Federal Bureau of Investigation, Uniform Crime Reporting Statistics, "State-by-State and National Crime Estimates by Year(s)," accessed at www.ucrdatatool.gov/Search/Crime/State/RunCrimeStatebyState.cfm, on Jan. 9, 2017; and U.S. Department of Justice, Federal Bureau of Investigation, Uniform Crime Reporting Program, "2015 Crime in the United States, Table 1: Crime in the United States by Volume and Rate per 100,000 Inhabitants, 1996-2015," accessed at https://ucr.fbi.gov/crime-in-the-u.s/2015/crime-in-the-u.s.-2015/tables/table-1, on Jan. 9, 2017.

106 Eliana Dockterman, "50 Years Ago, Doctors Called Domestic Violence 'Therapy,'" Time, Sept. 25, 2014, accessed at http://time.com/3426225/domestic-violence-therapy/, on Jan. 9, 2017.

107 Jennifer A. Bennice and Patricia A. Resick, "Marital Rape: History, Research, and Practice," Trauma, Violence, and Abuse 4, no. 3 (2003): 228-46.

108 University of Massachusetts, Amherst, "Research Finds That U.S. Murder Rate Suppressed by Improved Emergency Medical Response," July 31, 2002, accessed at www.umass.edu/newsoffice/article/research-finds-us-murder-rate-suppressed-improved-emergency-medical-response, on April 19, 2017; and U.S. Department of Justice, Federal Bureau of Investigation, Uniform Crime Reporting Program, "2015 Crime in the United States, Table 1: Crime in the United States by Volume and Rate per 100,000 Inhabitants, 1996-2015."

109 CDC, CDC WONDER Online Database, "Underlying Cause of Death 1999-2015."

110 Jarosz and VanOrman, "Accidental Poisoning Deaths—Mostly Drug Overdoses—Exceed Homicides of U.S. Young Adults."

111 Shannan Catalano et al., "Female Victims of Violence," U.S. Department of Justice, Office of Justice Programs, Bureau of Justice Statistics, Selected Findings NCJ 228356 (2009).

112 Mikel L. Walters, Jieru Chen, and Matthew J. Breiding, The National Intimate Partner and Sexual Violence Survey (NISVS): 2010 Findings on Victimization by Sexual Orientation (Atlanta: National Center for Injury Prevention and Control, CDC, 2013).

113 Matthew J. Breiding, Jieru Chen, and M.C. Black, Intimate Partner Violence in the United States–2010 (Atlanta: National Center for Injury Prevention and Control, CDC, 2014).

114 CDC, "Prevent Domestic Violence in Your Community," Oct. 3, 2016, accessed at www.cdc.gov/features/intimatepartnerviolence/, on April 6, 2017.

115 Institute of Medicine, "Epidemiology of Tobacco Use: History and Current Trends," in Ending the Tobacco Problem: A Blueprint for the Nation, ed. Richard J. Bonnie, Kathleen Stratton, and Robert B. Wallace (Washington, DC: The National Academies Press, 2007).

116 For cigarette smoking, we use 1965 to reflect ages 25-34 for the WWII generation due to data availability.

117 CDC, "Health Effects of Cigarette Smoking," Dec. 1, 2016, accessed at www.cdc.gov/tobacco/data_statistics/fact_sheets/health_effects/effects_cig_smoking/, on Jan. 9, 2017.

118 CDC, "Economic Trends in Tobacco," March 3, 2017, accessed at www.cdc.gov/tobacco/data_statistics/fact_sheets/economics/econ_facts/, on April 19, 2017.

119 Ahmed Jamal et al., "Current Cigarette Smoking Among Adults–United States, 2005-2015, Morbidity and Mortality Weekly Report 65, no. 44 (2016): 1205-11. These data are for all women ages 18 and older.

120 CDC, "Lesbian, Gay, Bisexual, and Transgender Persons and Tobacco Use," Feb. 28, 2017, accessed at www.cdc.gov/tobacco/disparities/lgbt/index.htm, on April 6, 2017.

121 CDC, "American Indians/Alaska Natives and Tobacco Use," March 1, 2017, accessed at www.cdc.gov/tobacco/disparities/american-indians/index.htm, on April 19, 2017; and Brian King, Terry Pechacek, and Peter Mariolis, Best Practices for Comprehensive Tobacco Control Programs – 2014 (Atlanta: U.S. Department of Health and Human Services, CDC, National Center for Chronic Disease Prevention and Health Promotion, Office on Smoking and Health, 2014).

122 Leonard J. Paulozzi, "Trends in Unintentional Drug Poisoning Deaths," statement delivered to the Committee on Energy and Commerce, Subcommittee on Oversight and Investigations, United States House of Representatives, Washington, DC, Oct. 24, 2007.

123 CDC, CDC WONDER Online Database, "Underlying Cause of Death 1999-2015."

124 Jarosz and VanOrman, "Accidental Poisoning Deaths—Mostly Drug Overdoses—Exceed Homicides of U.S. Young Adults."

125 J. Paul Johnson, "Seven Factors Reveal Why Women Don't Run for Office," Jan. 12, 2012, accessed at www.american.edu/media/news/20120113-Lawless-Gender-Gap-Politics.cfm, on April 19, 2017.

VISIT WWW.PRB.ORG TO FIND:

ARTICLES AND REPORTS. New data and analysis on topics as diverse as gender, reproductive health, environment, and race/ethnicity.

MULTIMEDIA. PRB has produced hundreds of cutting-edge videos with leading experts on topics as wide-ranging as the demographic dividend, climate change, immigration, HIV/AIDS, and nutrition. The Distilled Demographic series of short videos on population dynamics can help students learn demography's real-world application and impact.

PRB INSIGHTS. Sign up to receive e-mail announcements about new web content and PRB-sponsored seminars and briefings.

DATAFINDER. DataFinder is a searchable database of hundreds of indicators for thousands of places in the U.S. and around the world. In addition to data from PRB's *World Population Data Sheet* and other PRB data sheets, also included are data from the 2010 U.S. Census and the U.S. Census Bureau's American Community Survey. The site lets you easily create custom reports—rankings, trend graphs, bar charts, and maps to print, download, and share.

FOR EDUCATORS. Online lesson plans, and PRB's updated *Population Handbook.*

PRB NEWS AND EVENTS. Announcements of fellowship applications, workshops, and news about PRB's programs.

BECOME A MEMBER OF PRB

With new perspectives shaping public policies every day, you need to be well informed. As a member of the Population Reference Bureau, you will receive reliable information on United States and world population trends—properly analyzed and clearly presented in readable language. Each year you will receive two *Population Bulletins,* the annual *World Population Data Sheet*, and complimentary copies of special publications. We welcome you to join PRB today.

INDIVIDUAL	$50
LIBRARY	$75
CORPORATION	$300
LIFETIME MEMBERSHIP	$5,000

POPULATION REFERENCE BUREAU
1875 Connecticut Ave., NW, Suite 520
Washington, DC 20009-5728

For faster service, call 800-877-9881
Or visit www.prb.org
Or e-mail popref@prb.org
Or fax 202-328-3937

 @PRBData

Recent Population Bulletins

LOSING GROUND: YOUNG WOMEN'S WELL-BEING ACROSS GENERATIONS IN THE UNITED STATES

Gains in American young women's well-being rose rapidly for members of the Baby Boom generation, but stalled for subsequent generations. Social and structural barriers to young women's progress have contributed to persistently high poverty rates, a declining share of women in high-wage/high-tech jobs, a dramatic rise in women's incarceration rates,
and increases in maternal mortality and women's suicide.

In this *Population Bulletin*, PRB provides a broad overview of trends in young women's social, economic, and physical well-being over the past 50 years. PRB developed a new Index of Young Women's Well-Being to compare outcomes for present day young women (up to age 34) with young women in previous generations across 14 key social, economic, and health measures. The results show that the progress made by women of the Baby Boom generation (born 1946-1964) has stalled among women of Generation X (born 1965 to 1981) and the Millennial generation (born 1982 to 2002).

www.prb.org   @PRBData

POPULATION REFERENCE BUREAU

1875 Connecticut Avenue., NW   202 483 1100 PHONE
Suite 520   202 328 3937 FAX
Washington, DC 20009   popref@prb.org EMAIL

www.ingramcontent.com/pod-product-compliance
Lightning Source LLC
Chambersburg PA
CBHW060821290526
45792CB00005BB/1742